P9-BIN-135

"Jill Geisler's writing mirrors her compelling workshops. WORK HAPPY is a smart and substantive book that offers meaningful, practical advice to leaders at all levels in any organization."

—Robert M. Steele, Ph.D., Director, Janet Prindle Institute for Ethics, DePauw University

"Want to be a Great Boss? Then read WORK HAPPY, which explains with detailed work plans and assessment tools how to create a great work environment that gets results. Get one book for yourself—and another for your boss too. You'll both be happier for it!"

—Charlene Li, author of *Open Leadership* and co-author of *Groundswell*

"Want to love your job and reap the rewards of a productive staff? The secrets to achieve that are found in the pages of WORK HAPPY, as Jill Geisler challenges everything you know to manage yourself in order to lead others to success."

—Susana Schuler, Vice President of News, Raycom Media

"Jill has a talent for making great leadership seem slap-your-forehead simple. That's because her work in WORK HAPPY sits atop mountainous research and real-life experience that has been honed and scrutinized by some of the most exacting leaders around. The result is practical, rock-solid advice that you're ready to act on before she's done talking."

—Keith Woods, Vice President, NPR

"In a crisp, clear, upbeat style, Geisler cracks the code for what it takes to lead and to manage, even in times of change. Her experience as a leader, a coach, and a trainer of leaders comes through on every page. If you face the complex challenge of being your best as a leader and manager, WORK HAPPY puts a management guru by your side."

—Peggy Holman, author of *Engaging Emergence*

"Simply put, this book is a gift. A gift to any young manager in a new stretch assignment. A gift to any senior executive seeking to inspire a workforce. A gift to anyone driven to learn how to become a better leader. Jill Geisler's intelligence and warmth, captured within these pages, offers the reader an indispensable blend of best practices and comforting thoughts. She has created a safe place to think about becoming a better boss—which makes her something of a gift, too."

—Robert King, Senior Vice President, ESPN

"WORK HAPPY is an accessible, useful encyclopedia of managerial guidance artfully drawn from Jill Geisler's years as a master boss, learner, teacher, and coach. I just wish she had written it forty years ago....would have saved me lots of angst."

—Marty Linsky, Cambridge Leadership Associates, and faculty, Harvard Kennedy School

"Geisler, head of the Poynter Institute's leadership and management faculty and voice of the popular podcast *What Great Bosses Know*, has distilled years of management experience and study into this practical step-by-step guide to improving leadership skills. Covering topics including types of power, how to give and receive constructive feedback, coaching versus fixing, self-awareness and self-management, Geisler provides useful quizzes and assessments to help the reader translate the concepts into personal learning. This positive, useful work is sure to be a go-to manual for those new to management." —*Publishers Weekly*

"Jill Geisler has an uncanny ability to unravel the most complicated workplace problems and come up with creative solutions to resolve them." —Bob Schieffer, CBS News

Work Happy

What Great Bosses Know

Jill Geisler

CENTER STREET

New York Boston Nashville

Center Street
Hachette Book Group
237 Park Avenue
New York, NY 10017

www.centerstreet.com

Printed in the United States of America

RRD-C

Originally published in hardcover by Hachette Book Group.

First trade edition: January 2014

10   9   8   7   6   5   4   3   2

Center Street is a division of Hachette Book Group, Inc.
The Center Street name and logo are trademarks of Hachette Book Group, Inc.

The Hachette Speakers Bureau provides a wide range of authors for speaking events. To find out more, go to www.hachettespeakersbureau.com or call (866) 376-6591.

The publisher is not responsible for websites (or their content) that are not owned by the publisher.

The Library of Congress has cataloged the hardcover edition as follows:

Geisler, Jill.
    Work happy : what great bosses know / Jill Geisler.—1st ed.
       p. cm.
    ISBN 978-1-4555-0743-6
  1. Executive ability.   2. Supervision of employees.   3. Management.
4. Quality of work life.   I. Title.
    HD38.2.G45 2012
    658.4'09—dc23
                                                                 2011036201

ISBN 978-1-4555-4707-4 (pbk.)

For Neil, Noah, and Mac—
the soul of the "Real Me,"
who make work and *life happy*

ACKNOWLEDGMENTS

I believe in you.

This book is proof of the power of those words—spoken in many ways by the leaders, colleagues, and loved ones in my life. It's time to spotlight those speakers.

The leaders of the Poynter Institute—President Karen Dunlap, past President Jim Naughton, Dean Stephen Buckley, Senior Scholar Roy Peter Clark (writing guru extraordinaire), and Managing Director Butch Ward (my peerless, fearless teaching partner) have been nonstop sources of positive feedback. As the Director of Poynter Online, Julie Moos was my co-conspirator in the creation of the management columns and iTunes U podcasts that inspired this book. She is as gifted and generous an editor as she is a friend. Other Poynter colleagues helped with their talents and encouraged with their hearts. My sincere thanks to Ellyn Angelotti, Jacqui Banaszynski, Jessica Blais, Cathy Campbell, Aly Colón, Rick Edmonds,

Gregory Favre, Howard Finberg and the NewsU crew, Kenny Irby, Maria Jaimes, Kelly McBride, Regina McCombs, Bill Mitchell, Steve Myers, Paul Pohlman, Sara Quinn, David Shedden, Bob Steele, Mallary Tenore, Al Tompkins, Wendy Wallace, and Keith Woods for their work and their words. They and all my Poynter colleagues share a passion for excellence, not only in journalism that informs a democracy, but also in the practice and promise of leadership.

I'm grateful to my gracious Center Street editor, Kate Hartson, who knows the magic sentence every author needs to stay motivated—"You're a really good writer"—and to literary agents Jane Dystel and Miriam Goderich for bringing us together.

I am indebted to the many managers who have listened, learned, and laughed with me in seminars, workshops, and workplaces—and who reach out when they have successes to share or need a coaching ear. My special thanks to those unnamed but invaluable bosses whose 360-degree feedback excerpts in this book provided a clear window into the joys and challenges of leadership.

Looking back at my management career, my gratitude begins with Henry J. Davis and Carl Zimmermann, men who took a chance and didn't flinch when asked, "Are you crazy?" for promoting me. I hail (and hug) the indomitable Andy Potos, for years of adventures in broadcasting and community service—and for declaring, in his own understated way, that he thinks I'm "one hell of a leader." I'd bestow that title on Lil Kleiman, who co-led our newsroom with me and remains a guide star in my life. I also want to salute the many WITI-TV employees whose careers I touched, for embracing my guidance and enduring my mistakes.

Let me offer one last lesson. If you decide to write a book while continuing all other full-time work obligations—teaching, coaching, consulting, traveling—the secret to your success will be the support of remarkable friends who understand your inevitable anxieties and absences. May yours be as true and wise as my dear Kathy Potos and Rosalie Leib. You'd also benefit from a corps of Facebook friends worldwide, who send up a cheer each time you announce the completion of another chapter.

Most of all, this book's happy ending is a credit to the three men in my life: my best friend and husband, Neil Jaehnert, and our sons, Noah and MacNeil. From them, *I believe in you* is powerful—but their *I love you* is priceless.

Contents

Introduction

This book makes a bold promise: It will help grow great bosses and happy workplaces. Chapter by chapter, we'll take a professional and personal journey together. Because you are trusting me to be your guide, you deserve to know how I've come to be a leadership teacher and coach for countless managers. It's a story that begins years ago—with three little words: "Are you crazy?"

That was the warm response from the corporate brass when my boss promoted me to management. The home office couldn't fathom it. Why would the head of a major-market TV station hand its newsroom keys to an untested twenty-seven-year-old reporter whose only prior management experience was a high school summer job in a candy store?

This was high-stakes supervision. There was a multimillion-dollar budget to manage, legal, ethical, and regulatory issues to master, competitive strategy in media and marketing to devise, technology to deploy, unions to work with, contracts to negotiate, daily newscasts to oversee—and the small matter of the care and feeding of a staff of fifty, some of whose egos ranged in size from large to extra large.

Oh, and the year was 1978. Women news directors were a rarity back then. You can check the broadcast history books—or just watch *Mary Tyler Moore Show* reruns for proof. Maybe my boss *was* crazy. But where corporate saw insanity, he saw possibility.

He took a risk.

Each day, someone with power invests it in someone else, transforming the chosen person from staff to management, from producer to supervisor—and in the best cases, from follower to leader—all with the simple change of a title.

It's always a risk.

Most managers plunge in without benefit of training. It's a story that might sound familiar to you as a manager, or one you might face in the future if management is your goal. It goes like this:

You are a good performer, so you are tapped to lead a team. And then everything changes. What made you good at your craft isn't guaranteed to make you good at helping others excel. Even if you are smart, dedicated, and have a stellar work ethic, you have gaps in your supervisory skills, maybe some big ones. You make mistakes that can hurt employees, your company, and your own career. Like me, you can learn (and even teach) from those mistakes. You may get some limited training, depending on your organization. You might find mentors to guide you. You might invest in some books.

But which books? The store shelves are full of them—and you have precious little free time. You want—and deserve—*one* good book that brings together the most relevant and reliable advice for managers (or aspiring managers) at all stages of their careers. As someone who strives to be a great boss, you want to master the things the great ones do, and learn the secrets they know.

I promise to tell you.

So how do I know what makes work happy and what great bosses know? For the answer, I must take you back to my personal and professional adventure in leadership and the surprising outcome.

My boss's crazy big risk apparently paid off. I may have been too young, too inexperienced, and definitely not man enough to fit the traditional profile of '70s broadcast news director, but things actually worked out quite well. In a hard, competitive business where the average shelf life of a news director is two years, I ended up leading my team for more than two decades. Yes, twenty-plus years leading a team—building a culture and systems and growing a talented staff, some of whom set down roots and others who are doing distinguished work across the country today.

On top of that, our station went through five changes of ownership during my tenure. Each new set of overseers would conduct their due diligence, survey our performance—and choose to keep our management team intact. On every important score—revenue, ratings, award-winning quality, innovation, integrity, and employee engagement—we delivered.

That success came to the attention of the Poynter Institute, a highly respected nonprofit school in St. Petersburg, Florida. It specializes in sharing best practices through programs that are innovative, interactive, and engaging. Starting in the early '90s, I was invited to serve as occasional guest faculty for the institute's management seminars. It was there that I began to frame and give form to the management ideas and techniques I'd adopted or abandoned. I shared my successes and failures in ways that helped other supervisors improve their performance. And we laughed a lot. I consider that a vital part of teaching, learning, and leading. (It also explains why this book is titled *Work Happy.*)

I must have done something right. In 1998, Poynter invited me to leave my newsroom (which by then had grown to about a hundred employees) and join the institute's small and special faculty. While I had absolutely loved being a vice president of news in a demanding industry, my heart told me it was time for a new challenge.

Helping managers has been my life and passion ever since. I teach and coach leaders around the world, write advice columns for bosses in all professions, and produce *What Great Bosses Know* podcasts that have had millions of downloads on iTunes U and led to this book.

Along the way, I earned a master's degree in leadership studies and continuously devoured business management literature, especially information that is research-based. Frankly, there's an abundance of untested opinions and frothy folktales about leadership out there; my training as a journalist makes me extremely picky about citing authoritative sources.

That's part of how I know what great bosses know—but there's more. I have a priceless pipeline of information about the best and worst behaviors of bosses and insights into happy workplaces. Let me explain:

When I took responsibility for our institute's leadership and management programs, I introduced a new element to our teaching—something that improved our effectiveness and, according to the participants, became the most valuable part of their management learning experience. I developed our own version of what social scientists call a multirater feedback instrument, commonly known as "360-degree feedback." The managers I teach solicit feedback from their bosses, from fellow managers, and from employees. I have read thousands, yes thousands, of these reports, taking in detailed descriptions of what the best bosses know and do. The feedback also speaks candidly about what bosses need to do better.

I've selected some powerful statements from those feedback reports to share with you in this book, because they represent the voices of real people talking about real bosses. Don't expect to read the names of folks who sent or received this feedback. I care deeply about the managers I teach, and neither generous bribes nor enhanced interrogation methods would persuade me to violate their privacy. This book is about great bosses, not great gossip. In some cases, I've done very light editing of the feedback for clarity, brevity, and grammar, or to substitute the word "manager" or "boss" for a person's specific title or name—but never to alter the meaning or impact of the praise or criticism.

There is one name I'll share openly when reporting on managerial missteps: *my own*. As I like to tell managers, I teach from my mistakes so you won't make them, too.

So let's get started—with the focus on *you* and what the people you work with would say if they were asked to evaluate your skills as a boss. Here's our goal: Whatever they say today will pale in comparison to the praise you'll hear in the very near future—after you've "graduated" from the lessons in this book and see how the words "work" and "happy" can flourish side by side. Let the fun begin.

SECTION ONE

All About You

How Bosses Become Great

CHAPTER 1

The Challenges and Joys of Management—a Reality Check

Imagine this: I've just handed you a manila folder. You are nervous. You've never looked at feedback like this before. It's a report card, but without numeric or letter grades. Instead, it is page upon page of candid comments about your strengths and weaknesses as a manager, written by those who interact with you regularly. No wonder you're a little queasy. You truly want to be a great boss—but you know it's not easy, not with the daily challenges that surface like a never-ending game of Whac-A-Mole. You can't please everyone, right? You take a deep breath. You open the folder and begin to read. You see this:

She is a great boss and even people outside our team look to her for advice, motivation, and answers. She praises our smallest of achievements, points out our mistakes without making a big deal of them, and listens and helps if we are struggling with something. Unlike most bosses, she recognizes that the personal affects the professional.

Perhaps you see this:

His enthusiasm is contagious. People enjoy working for him because he isn't jaded or cynical. He inspires people to work harder. His judgment is respected by both his staff and his supervisors. He is loyal to the company, yet not afraid to speak his mind.

How about this:

He has a fantastic ability to listen to criticism and act positively on that criticism. He is good at selecting the right person for the job, and is genuinely liked by his colleagues. He inspires confidence and brings out the best in people. He is good at working as part of a large team with many conflicting ideas and agendas. It's fun to be at work when he is the boss.

Wow. What powerful praise. How are you feeling now? Surprised? Perhaps. Delighted? You should be. That's how the managers who received that very real feedback responded. I was there when they read it in my management development seminar. I saw their relief—and downright joy. But as you might imagine, not every boss gets such glowing reviews. I've had to deliver folders bearing candid criticism of managerial shortcomings.

Imagine that your report contains messages like this:

He comes across as combative and abrasive to other departments and staff. There are times he fails to share his wealth of knowledge with his staff and if he is not available for help it can cause problems.

Or this:

He doesn't share important details with employees in a timely manner. Too many announcements start with, "You've probably heard by now that . . . ," and no, I haven't heard anything.

Or this:

I understand the pressure she has, but that's no excuse to treat some people like crap.

Ouch. What a painful wake-up call, right?

I suspect that if this were your feedback, you may have had no idea that some people viewed you this way. That's often the case. It hurts to discover a perception of you that, accurate or not, exists in your workplace. Your challenge is to take the knowledge from the hard knock and respond with the right plan. Think of it as a bruise—a wound that can heal with no permanent scar, provided you know how to treat it.

While most organizations use some form of performance evaluation for employees, chances are yours doesn't include such detailed feedback—positive or negative. Don't worry. You aren't destined to blindly blunder on. Not at all. In the pages ahead, I'll help you find ways to assess your performance and potential as a leader, and, most of all, provide concrete tools to help you improve—all toward your goal of being a great boss.

Let's start with a quick self-assessment—and a request that for now, you just give me your best guess. Take a look at the box titled "Check Yourself: Twelve Core Management Competencies." Read each one of the twelve and jot down a few words you would use to describe your own performance. It could be anything from "I excel at this" to "I need help with this one" to "Haven't dealt with this yet"—just some brief, honest thoughts.

CHECK YOURSELF: TWELVE CORE MANAGEMENT COMPETENCIES

1. Maintaining and raising quality _____

2. Developing and improving systems _____

3. Coaching employee performance _____

4. Communicating across the organization _____
    _____

5. Collaborating across the organization _____
    _____

6. Resolving conflicts _____

7. Building employee motivation _____

8. Leading with emotional intelligence _____

9. Building teams and team performance _____
    _____

10. Managing change _____

11. Managing your time and priorities _____

12. Working with ethics and integrity _____

Next step: Take a second look at the list. Now imagine that you have asked your boss, other managers, and several people you supervise to jot down *their* thoughts about your work in each of these areas.

- What are the *best* comments you might hope for?
- What are the *worst* words you might fear?

In truth, this list barely scratches the surface of the many skills managers need and the values leaders can and should bring to their roles. It doesn't begin to address the nuances of leadership and the many daunting management situations we'll address in future chapters.

But I have good news for you: To be a great boss, you don't have to be perfect.

Let me repeat that: To be a great boss, you don't have to be perfect.

Remember those managers who were delighted by the powerfully positive quotes they read about themselves? Each of them also had some weaknesses they needed to shore up. What about the bosses with the negative notes? They weren't ogres or losers. In fact, they had other skills and strengths their colleagues truly valued. But the feedback helped them see how some of their behaviors were getting in the way of their success.

You don't have to be perfect. But you must have a commitment to understanding and leveraging your strengths, as well as recognizing and filling your gaps. I believe your path to becoming a great boss should begin with an honest reckoning of the high degree of difficulty that comes with the role of manager. After all, this supervisory stuff is hard work.

So, it's time for a reality check about your life, distilled into a Top Five list.

THE TOP FIVE DAILY CHALLENGES FOR BOSSES

1. Managers disappoint people every day.

It happens in many small ways and a few big ones. You critique and correct people's work. You give assignments and promotions that many employees want but only a few can get. You enforce rules that people don't appreciate. You schedule staffers to shifts they don't prefer. You approve some ideas over others and apportion scarce resources. You pass judgment on conflicts. And those are just the everyday events. You also navigate the less routine but truly tough situations: cutting overtime, salaries, benefits—or staff.

2. Managers push people out of their comfort zones.

In today's changing organizations, you are requiring that people learn new skills and work across old boundaries. You are pressing them to adapt to fresh tools and frightening technologies. You're shaking up traditional systems and processes. You're expecting staff to increase productivity while maintaining quality. You may be asking veteran workers to report to younger managers—or you may be one of those young supervisors tasked with managing older staffers as well as your old friends. And you're expected to keep morale high while they're dealing with all this discomfort.

3. Managers are routinely caught in the middle.

There's pressure on you from all directions. From above, there's a push for you to meet specific budgetary and production goals and to hold people accountable. Nearby, you have fellow managers pressing you to step up, step in, or step back—depending on the day or the work at hand. From the troops, there's the expectation that you will defend them and be the advocate for their ideas, issues, and ambitions to the powers-that-be. In that middle spot, you're a translator, negotiator, and shock absorber as you attempt to satisfy and reconcile those diverse, conflicting demands.

4. Managers can't always tell people what they want to know.

People look to you for information. They count on you to keep them informed because knowledge is indeed power. But even if you pride yourself on keeping people in the loop, you have a responsibility to handle sensitive business and staff matters with discretion. It leads to frustrating scenarios like this: Staff members are griping to you about an underperformer on the team. They don't know that you're already taking action about that person. You'd like to prove that you're truly on the case—but you can't broadcast the contents of an employee's personnel file. So you talk in vague terms, which may not satisfy the complainers. Nor can you delve into details when people ask about sensitive business plans, legal actions, or competitive strategies—even though they affect their workplace. As a boss, you are constantly balancing two conflicting goals: to be as transparent as possible, feeding employees' reasonable hunger to know what's going on—and to be trusted steward of a business's proprietary information.

5. Managers make mistakes.

When your days are filled with decisions, chances are you'll occasionally stumble—or even truly screw up. The reasons vary, but here are the most common: In the moment, you may be impatient or overly cautious, too trusting or too skeptical. You may be underinformed, underprepared, blindsided, or even biased. You may simply forget something or someone. Your math may be off. Whatever the cause, you mess up. How you manage the fallout of your fallibility will determine whether you keep—and even *build*—your credibility. Yes, I said *build*.

I believe it's healthy to get these challenges on the table. Naming them is the first step to taming them. Your next step is to develop strategies for navigating these challenges and emerging a smarter and stronger boss.

Let's tackle each one.

DO'S AND DON'TS OF THE TOP FIVE MANAGEMENT CHALLENGES

1. Disappointing people daily

Don't: Fall into the trap of thinking that since you can't please everyone, it doesn't pay to try. Don't write off people as whiners or malcontents when they complain to you. Conversely, don't sidestep this challenge by sugarcoating bad news or dodging tough conversations.

Do: Assume that building trust with staff is paramount. You do it by letting them know the standards and values that drive your decisions. You do that person-to-person, day after day. There's evidence that even when people don't like the outcome of a management decision, they will react less negatively and be more accepting if they believe *the process by which it happened* was fair.

Columbia Business School professor Joel Brockner has studied the concept of "process fairness" in organizations. Writing in the *Harvard Business Review*, he noted three key factors that influence employees' perception of whether a decision is made through a fair process:

- How much input employees feel they have. Are their opinions solicited and considered?
- How they perceive decisions are made. Are they consistent and driven by facts, not by personal bias? Is the process transparent? Can mistakes be corrected?
- How managers behave in delivering and carrying out the decision. Do they act with respect? Do they listen, explain, and empathize?

No one likes criticism, but it pays to give a hearing to people who push back responsibly. It can help you understand their perceptions, and give you opportunities not only to address them, but also to build trust.

2. Pushing people out of their comfort zones

Don't: Bulldoze or bully employees, thinking that shock therapy will change their thinking. You may achieve a little short-term change but create long-term problems. As you'll learn later in this book, terror is rarely a good motivator. At the same time, don't back down just because rocking the boat is making everyone a little queasy. Few managers today are hired to keep things completely static. Change is a constant part of management life.

Do: Be smart and persistent. Custom-calibrate your pressure to the individual. Does this person respond best to a shove or a shoulder tap? Researchers who have studied managerial assertiveness say that bosses often come on too strong and get in the way of their own effectiveness. To a lesser degree, some are too wimpy and lose respect. The key is to be moderately assertive most of the time, so even-keeled about it that people barely notice. But you must be prepared and able to power up or down based on the situation and other people involved.

3. Getting caught in the middle

Don't: Play bosses, fellow managers, and employees off one another. Don't diss your own managers or distance yourself from their decisions by telling your team that they came from the "powers-that-be"—unless you are struggling in a truly dysfunctional environment. If you find yourself needing to consistently dissociate yourself from the decisions of others, it's a signal that you are working in the wrong organization.

Do: Serve as the savvy advocate for your staff. Become adept at "managing up"—keeping your bosses in the loop about the progress and potential of your people, along with their big victories and vexing challenges. Build alliances with fellow managers. Set an example of collaboration with them that your team can follow.

4. Being unable to communicate completely

Don't: Hoard information as a way of building your empire. Don't develop a reputation for sharing mainly with people you like, for trafficking in rumor and gossip, or for being inconsistent in your communication. Don't assume people know which types of information managers are ethically and legally bound to protect.

Do: Commit to sharing appropriate information generously. At the same time, educate people about the kind of communication you won't spread freely: sensitive business strategies or data that could help competitors, employee personnel files or private health issues. Strive to make certain that the people who are most affected by bad news don't learn it secondhand. Deliver it personally. In the end, if you develop a reputation for being a proactive, forthright, and trustworthy communicator, people are more likely to understand when you say, "I'm sorry, but this is something I can't discuss," or "Take my word for it, this situation is being addressed, but I'm not able to say more at this time."

5. Making mistakes

Don't: Assume you must always appear smarter than your staff. Don't think you'll look weak if you ask for their advice or admit you don't know something. Don't cling to a shaky position just to save face. Don't hold yourself to a different standard of accountability than your staff. Don't fear that apologizing for a mistake undercuts your standing as a leader.

Do: Recognize that the way you respond to your employees' mistakes shapes the way they view yours. If you're a hothead or slow to forgive, your actions will come back to haunt you when *you* stumble. When you screw up, apologize sincerely and specifically. Use the lessons from your lapses to help you and others grow. It's easy to teach from your victories; it takes guts and confidence to reveal what you learned from your failures.

Here's a bonus "do" for you: Do believe that it's worth the effort to become a great boss.

Permit me to bring in another voice to remind you why it's worth it. Let's peek into another one of those feedback folders I told you about. The boss is an editor at a major U.S. newspaper; the feedback is from a reporter on her team. Bear in mind that relationships between reporters and editors can be dicey. Sharp journalists have a habit of challenging authority. They like to wrangle with bosses over creativity and control. Yet this reporter wrote:

What can you say about an editor you trust completely, who you know would do anything for you and your story, who inspires you, and who makes work not seem like work at all? If I could get her to be the editor of my life, I'd be a better person.

I wish you could have seen the way that editor simply beamed, reading those words. She was actually embarrassed to have received such a love note. She had approached her work as a boss very seriously, but didn't dream she was having that kind of impact—not just with that staffer, but with others who described her high standards and great skills, her contagious optimism and sense of humor. One simply suggested: *Clone her.*

Keep in mind, that editor faced the same daily challenges that all managers do, but she knew how to navigate them successfully. You too can have that kind of impact. And as they say in TV infomercials, "Wait, there's more!" Since we've examined the top five daily challenges managers face each day, let's give equal attention to the remarkably positive side of the leadership ledger. Let's look at why being a boss is a wonderful opportunity and occupation. Here's another Top Five list:

The Five Key Rewards of Management

1. You leverage your expertise and develop new skills.

As a manager, you have the opportunity to take what you've already learned—and excelled in—to another level. Your organization looks to you to take that knowledge and talent and share it with others. But you're not just an in-house expert on the work you once did as an employee. Now you shift from using a narrow focus to a wide-angle lens. You engage in continuous learning about your industry and its future, your people and their needs, plus the fiscal, legal, technical, political, and social aspects of leadership. Simply put, you have the chance to move from smart doer to wise leader.

2. You have the power to build a workplace culture.

Think about that. You may be leading a tiny team or the whole organization, but you have the ability to shape "the way we do things around here"—the workplace culture. It's about structure and processes, systems and relationships. It's about the heroes people tell stories about and the villains they want to vanquish. It's about a happy workplace. It's about values. As one of my favorite researchers on corporate culture, MIT's Edgar Schein, teaches, organizational culture is built on assumptions that run so deep the team takes them for granted and they operate accordingly. (If this sounds intimidating, don't worry, we'll focus on building cultures later in the book.) As a boss, you can make certain that a mission statement isn't simply words or wishes—it's values in action.

3. You help people succeed.

Where once you defined success by your personal achievements, you now measure it through the accomplishments of others. Your coaching, feedback, and mentoring pays off as your employees reach their goals and yours. You set standards, evaluate performance, hire for talent and character, and celebrate victories. Their wins are your joy. And as you help people depend less and less on you for their decisions, you get the satisfaction of watching them do the right thing for the right reasons—on their own.

4. You design strategy and guide execution.

This is the part that puts your brain into high gear. You scout for opportunities, anticipate challenges, and identify needed changes. While you're keeping an eye on the quality of today's work, you're also looking down the road. What's next? What's better? How can we work smarter and outperform our competition? What are our customers saying and how do we respond? You turn that intelligence into overall strategy, then turn strategy into ground-level tactics. You take part in building the playbook and positioning your team for wins.

5. You manage meaning and share a vision.

The importance of this is sometimes overlooked or taken for granted, but great bosses understand the power of putting things in perspective. You find the right words to celebrate victories, recover from setbacks, or crank up energy and enthusiasm. You calm fears or sound appropriate alarm bells. You put form to feelings and make it safe for people to talk about things that matter. There are many ways to look at any situation, and some may be counterproductive. That's why people look to you to frame things credibly, helpfully, and even inspirationally. You are the person who helps people make sense of things, understand the most important goals, and pave the road ahead.

There's another reward of management—especially if you're a great boss. Every now and then you discover that someone chooses words like these to describe *you*:

Integrity. Dedication. Consistency. Maturity. Full under-standing of the possibilities of the product. Compassion, both professionally and personally. Vision. An ability to overlook frustrating minutiae and maintain clarity on the big picture. And one big sense of humor.

And that's one big reminder why learning to become a great boss is well worth the effort. You can be the reason employees are happy at work—and so are you.

Let's get started on your leadership journey. For every tough reality of management and every joyful opportunity, I promise to share insights and advice you can put to use immediately.

CHAPTER 2

What Employees Never Forget— and Never Forgive (and Why They Don't Like Your Evil Twin)

Q: If there are no perfect bosses, and even the best have some quirks—what is it that truly sets the great bosses apart?

A: They possess something that overshadows their short-comings: the trust of people who choose to follow them.

Social scientists who study trust define it as confidence—in the face of risk—that the other party will do what's right by us. With bosses we trust, we lower our guard and raise our expectations of positive outcomes. We may go the extra mile and let go of irritations or disappointments. We believe good things will happen.

Trust isn't a gift; it is an earned benefit. Bosses have to work for it and never take it for granted. As a leader, you earn trust when people see a direct, positive connection between the values that matter to them and the things you do.

Let's illustrate it by comparing the feedback of two managers, let's just call them "A" and "B." Both of these bosses were given credit by their employees for their intelligence and their professional knowledge. But as you can see from the feedback, there's a vast difference in their relationships with their teams:

Manager A:
The atmosphere she creates is not one of trust, encouragement, or collaboration. She is so competitive and condescending that she is completely unable to translate her other skills into any sort of mentoring or leadership...She is tremendously vague about what she wants, not at all open to other people's ideas, and not at all open to feedback on her own.

Manager B:
His strengths as a supervisor center on the climate of trust and support he has created in the department... He's extraordinarily candid—even about what he sees as his own faults—and that is disarming. He also works incredibly hard and cares very much. His combination of traits inspires an almost protective feeling—something pretty close to devotion—from his staff. Even in a very self-motivating group, he has a knack of motivating people to work harder, just to please him.

Manager A's feedback demonstrates why it takes far more than deep knowledge of one's profession to be effective in managing others. This boss was given credit in her feedback report for being intelligent and energetic. But her actions were so off-putting that she lost the support of her team. More specifically, her behaviors got in the way of building trust.

Manager B's feedback was the stuff of great bosses. His values mirrored those of his team, and he walked his talk. Colleague after colleague said similar things about him. This great boss valued quality in process, people, and problem-solving. He made a conscious decision to weigh everything he did, every interaction with staff, against those values—and act accordingly. You can, too.

Just know that building trust takes time. You "audition" for the role of "trusted leader" whenever you connect with employees. In addition, there are pivotal moments in which bosses make indelible impressions for better—or worse. So it's important to identify key trust builders and trust busters, the things employees never forget and never forgive. Let's look at three of each:

THREE THINGS EMPLOYEES NEVER FORGET

1. My boss apologized to me when he or she was in the wrong.

As I told you in chapter 1, every boss makes mistakes. When it happens, some bosses are tempted to downplay it, make light of it, or acknowledge it without apology. A manager once told me he felt he couldn't apologize for a bad decision because he'd lose face in front of his team. I counseled him that he was only compounding his error. When a powerful person apologizes, the payback is credibility—provided the mea culpa is specific and sincere. Not a watered-down "If someone believes I was mistaken, or took offense, then I apologize." (Translation: "I don't think it's a big deal, but you do, so I'm paying lip service here.") Not a passive-voice pass-the-buck "Mistakes were made and I regret that." (Translation: "I can't bring myself to say it's my fault, but I don't like the mess.") Your apology should describe the wrong, take personal responsibility for it—and also make clear why it's unlikely to happen again. Example: "Yesterday I said you dropped the ball on this assignment. I was wrong. I forgot that I had asked you to put it on hold. I apologize for criticizing you for something that was my error. You have my word I'll keep better project notes from now on."

> For bonus credibility points: Deliver the apology at the scene of the crime—meaning, if you delivered criticism in front of others, deliver your self-criticism in front of the same people.

2. My boss reacted to a truly boneheaded error of mine with remarkable wisdom.

Good employees occasionally do dumb things. Not life-threatening or criminal, just stupid and rare. Great bosses don't ignore or avenge, they help people learn from them. They investigate the cause, assess the damage, express disappointment, look for the lesson, teach the lesson, and expect better. They're smart enough to know just how long good staffers need to stew and second-guess themselves—which they inevitably do. They also know when such behaviors become counterproductive. That's when they apply a boss's benediction to close the case. (Note that I'm talking about good employees here, not chronic underperformers. That's another challenge—and gets its own chapter!)

> For bonus credibility points: Look back and laugh about it with the employee when the time is right—but only if that employee doesn't see it as teasing or torment.

3. My boss responded to something personal and important to me—a joy or a tragedy—with empathy and encouragement.

Great bosses understand that when something of great consequence happens in an employee's life, they have the power to enhance the joy or ameliorate a little of the pain. Weddings, funerals, childbirth—those are the obvious ones. But the right response from the boss when employees win awards or get new certifications, when their children or partners experience success, when their parents get sick or their pets get lost, can make a lasting impression on a staffer. When I conducted an industry survey on work-life balance issues, I was struck by the deep appreciation expressed for bosses who understood this. Witness this comment:

> *I'm the caretaker for a seriously ill family member. My supervisor is fully supportive in helping me juggle my*

schedule to meet the needs created by the illness. He lets me know that family is the number one priority and does not make me feel guilty. That relieves me of additional pressures. I make sure I give back in return.

Take special note of that last line. You see more than just appreciation; you see payback.

> For bonus credibility points: In tough times as well as celebrations, never underestimate the importance of a message of support from the boss—especially a handwritten note.

Now that we've shared three unforgettable things, it's time for the flip side:

THREE THINGS EMPLOYEES NEVER FORGIVE

1. My boss lies.

For employees, falsehoods take many forms. There's the basic, provable untruth. But there are also promises that aren't kept, apparent inconsistencies in words and actions, and inflated—then dashed—expectations. While it is a fact of life that bosses disappoint people in some way every day, doing so by consciously dissembling shouldn't be one of them. The temptation to deliver even good news ("Next year's budget was just approved and you're set for a 5 percent raise on your anniversary") must be tempered by the business realities that could make you a liar. ("Raises got cut after the first-quarter results came in lower than projected. I never expected this.") That's why it is important for bosses to weigh their words carefully and never underestimate how important communication is as a management skill.

> For minus credibility points: Tell a lie that deflects blame from you onto others. It's a trust killer.

2. My boss takes or gets credit for the staff's work or ideas.

When a manager gets the spotlight and doesn't widen it out to include the team, it's a real problem. Positive feedback is always in short supply in organizations—just ask employees. That's why great bosses not only give credit to their team members, they make certain their own leaders know who deserves it most. They never miss an opportunity to get their employees' good work on the radar screen and aren't intimidated when staff members look like heroes. Further, they're smart enough to recognize the limits of their own memories—so when writing a report or memo that acknowledges the people behind a big success, they have a second set of eyes double-check it before publication. That protects them from missing even one name, one individual who may forever remember the sting of being forgotten.

> For minus credibility points: Assume that good work speaks for itself and the careful distribution of credit is nothing more than office politics, which you disdain.

3. My boss is one person around the troops and another person in the company of his/her own superiors.

You'll hear me say many times in this book that you are always "on stage" as a boss. People watch you closely and read meaning into your actions, rightly or wrongly. There are two situations in which managers are under extreme scrutiny by staff. One is infrequent: when there's a crisis. But the other is so commonplace that managers may not be aware of it: when they're operating around their superiors.

Employees, with acutely sensitive hypocrisy detectors activated, watch you very closely as you interact with the brass. If you're slightly more diplomatic or dressed a little sharper for an occasion, that's okay—your people will probably just tease you about that. What really matters to them is your overall authenticity. They want to know you are conveying the same messages upward that you do to the troops. Are you advocating for them? Are you shining a light on things that matter to them? When you're mingling with the powers-that-be, are you representing the team or just you? If you give your staff reason to think you're flying solo, they'll brand you as untrustworthy.

For minus credibility points: Bad-mouth your bosses to the troops, distance yourself from upper management decisions, but fail to speak truth to power when you have the opportunity.

BEWARE OF YOUR EVIL TWIN

As an aspiring great boss, you're on your way to racking up some "unforgettables" and making certain to avoid the "unforgivables." But it's not as easy as it seems, because while you may be trying your best, you have an Evil Twin who's working against you—but you don't even know it.

Where do our Evil Twins come from? They spring to life through the perception of others, who see things through their own lenses, not ours.

Here's what I mean: Managers know what they believe in, what they aspire to be, and what their intentions are in their everyday interactions with staff. But what they carry in their hearts and minds isn't necessarily apparent to others.

In the minds of bosses and employees, the qualities of great managers are clear. They'll name things like:

- Intelligence
- High standards
- Integrity
- Determination
- Vision

But when I hear about management flaws and shortcomings—situations in which bosses disappoint their employees—I rarely hear about behaviors or traits that are the *opposite* of those good qualities.

To illustrate, I've listed the opposites on the chart below:

Quality	Opposite Quality
Intelligence	Ignorance
High standards	Low standards
Integrity	Sleaze
Determination	Weak-willed
Vision	Shortsightedness

The flawed managers I hear about are rarely described by those opposite terms. Instead, I hear Evil Twin terms, which are the flip side of some otherwise wonderful traits. Sometimes it is a good characteristic taken to extremes. Or it's a good intention that was executed badly.

Here's what that looks like:

Leadership Characteristic	Evil Twin
Intelligence	Too smart for own good
High standards	Impossible to satisfy
Integrity	Holier-than-thou
Determination	Ruthlessness
Vision	Delusion

In my work with managers, I've seen it time and again. Well-intentioned bosses discover that what they *think* they are saying and doing isn't what their team perceives.

Some examples:

- A manager who cares deeply about quality control and rooting out errors sees herself as "vigilant." Staffers see her Evil Twin, "relentlessly negative."
- A boss with a lot of tasks to accomplish each day and who keeps his conversations brief and brisk sees himself as "efficient and businesslike." Employees see his Evil Twin, "impatient and unfriendly."
- A supervisor who wants staffers to feel they have a voice in daily decision-making and asks for lots of input before acting sees himself as "collaborative." Staffers see his Evil Twin, "indecisive."

Not a single one of those bosses woke up each morning, thinking, "How can I make someone's life really crummy today?" None intended to develop a flawed reputation. In their heads, they were doing the right things, just as I believe most bosses try to do. But their Evil Twins were working against them.

Sometimes, we are introduced to our Evil Twins long after those shady siblings have begun doing harm. During annual reviews, for example, we might be smacked in the gut with a revelation about our shortcomings and about people's frustrations with the way we're running the show. How, we wonder, could this be? Why didn't anyone bring this up before?

It is then that we learn how hard it is for the people who work for us to speak truth to power. If they are seeing your Evil Twin, "dictator," while you are positive you are "strong leader," chances are they won't be comfortable challenging you.

MEET MY EVIL TWIN

It's time for me to share my Evil Twin confession. As a television news director, I met my dark doppelgänger in my newsroom early on a snowy Wisconsin morning. This is what happened:

A big winter storm was looming, so I followed my usual custom when rallying the troops for coverage. If I asked them to show up for work at 3 a.m., I would make sure to be in the newsroom at least an hour earlier. I'd park myself in some conspicuous place, ready to lend a hand. In my mind, I was the "News Director Who Wouldn't Ask You to Do Something I Wouldn't Do."

But one day, a news anchor said, "You know, we wouldn't screw up if you didn't come for every storm." As it turns out, my Evil Twin—the "News Director Who Didn't Really Trust the Crew Even Though They'd Covered Storms a Bazillion Times"—was who they saw.

That anchor was a respected leader in the newsroom with whom I had a trusting relationship, so she felt free to be candid with me, thank goodness. It gave me the chance to explain myself more clearly to her and to others—to change their perception and even some of my own behaviors. In the future, I would be there to lead when it mattered or I'd delegate and let them run the show, and we'd all know why.

I never forgot that lesson—and it's become a core part of my leadership and management teaching and coaching, because every boss can understand and act on it.

Now let's shake off the snow and get back to you and your team. We'll look at an everyday Evil Twin challenge: your reputation as an accessible supervisor. It's a clear illustration of the gap between your good intentions and the way people may misread you. It's the perfect opportunity to illustrate the work you need to do to close the gap—and build trust that's critical to being a great boss.

THE MYTH OF THE OPEN DOOR

You probably pride yourself on having an open-door policy. Many managers do. You want people who report to you to feel free to walk right in and share what's on their minds. Why is it, then, that a recent survey by the training firm Leadership IQ found that 66 percent of employees say they have too little interaction with their supervisors? Why do I hear the identical complaint from employees wherever I teach—not enough feedback from bosses and insufficient opportunities to give them input? Why might it come as a surprise to bosses like you who want your open door to be the gateway to great working relationships?

It's a matter of focus. Since *some* staffers stroll right into your workspace to chat, you see it as proof that your policy works. But that logic is built on counting *those who show up* rather than those who don't. And it's easy for you to assume that since your door is "always open," those who don't stop by are satisfied with the status quo.

It can be a real surprise when managers discover that to some staff members, the open-door mantra is a myth. Good employees feel shut out. It's a trust buster you don't want and it's your challenge to fix.

Four Things That Fuel the Myth of the Open Door

1. Your door is open—but people aren't comfortable making the approach.

It can be hard for managers, especially extroverts, to grasp why employees would pass up a standing offer to visit. But employees have their reasons. They may be introverts who don't relish initiating the conversations. (We'll take an in-depth look at these personality types in chapter 7.) Some staffers may assume that a visit to the boss's turf is reserved for problems or conversations on topics that are remarkable, not routine. Some may fear that stopping by with a concern, comment—or, heaven forbid, a compliment—could brand them as a troublemaker, showboat, or suck-up.

2. Your door is open—but you haven't been clear about chain of command and communication.

This happens when there's a layer of managers between you and staff. Employees may want to talk to you, but they fear they'll be accused of doing an end run around their immediate supervisors. Unless you make your protocol clear to the whole staff, employees may hang back, fearing retribution from their bosses.

3. Your door is open—but you send lots of mixed signals.

Bosses are always on stage. People watch you and read meaning—perhaps accurate, perhaps wildly off-base—into your actions. If you're away from your desk or home base a lot, people may assume you're inaccessible. When you're there, they may scope out who spends time with you and surmise those folks are the "in" group—and they're "out." Or when you tell a would-be visitor that you're busy, but you don't close the loop—that is, tell them when you *can* meet—they may feel like offenders or the offended when you intended neither.

4. Your door is open—but visits aren't worth the effort.

If your employees believe you multitask your way through conversations with them, if you lecture instead of listen, if you listen but don't follow through, or if you routinely start appointments late and end them early, you're sending a powerful message: Your open door is an invitation to frustration. Nothing demonstrates that as clearly as this feedback, given to an otherwise respected manager with a habit of answering email while people talked with him:

> *I fully respect that you say your door is always open, but maybe it would be better if you sometimes ask for some space to do your work. I think most people would understand that. It is very important for me to feel that you are fully present when I walk into your office and have to ask you something.*

In the boss's mind, he was "Mr. Super Busy but Always Here for You," while others saw his Evil Twin, "Mr. Always Here but Too Super Busy for Me."

If you want your open door to be real—not a myth—here's what you can do:

• **Assume it's your responsibility** to reach out to those who don't approach you. Some people may never knock on your door but still want to connect.

• **Help people know** the range of conversations they can bring your way—from major to minor, so they know the "password" to your place.

• **Have a clear understanding** with your managers and staff about the definition of an "end run." Build a culture that encourages people to solve problems at the lowest level and talk with their immediate supervisor before coming to you.

That doesn't mean people shouldn't have great conversations with you about ideas and issues; they should know you'll be transparent with their bosses about those conversations. (The exception: highly sensitive situations in which the immediate supervisor may be the source of a serious problem and confidentiality may be called for.)

• **Close the loop.** You can't say yes to every person who pops in with, "Got a minute?" But "No, not now" doesn't close the loop. Try my favorite reply: "I have a minute, but I bet your issue deserves more. How about this afternoon at 3:30, when we can really talk?"

Finally, what's the best way to deal with Evil Twins? How can you discover and disown yours, without waiting for a snowstorm or a not-so-hot annual review? Try **transparency**.

How to Build Transparency and Disown Your Evil Twin

- Don't assume that people can read your mind or that your actions speak for themselves.
- Explain your intentions. Be clear.
- Don't hesitate to share the "why" behind your decisions.
- Make certain your deputies feel free to warn you when something you're about to do has the potential to be taken the wrong way.
- Cultivate your top performers to become your candid advisors. They see how your leadership affects the team, and have more confidence than most to call you out when necessary.
- Thank anyone who has the courage to warn you that your Evil Twin is in the room.

The Million-Dollar Question

If you want to be certain you're on the right track as a manager, be open to feedback on your performance as a boss. You can do this whether or not your organization uses any formal feedback system. You need to seek it out.

But, as a Competent and Caring Boss in Search of Constructive Feedback, how do you make certain people don't mistakenly see an Evil Twin—a Self-Absorbed, Insecure Supervisor Seeking Compliments or Consolation?

It's all in how you ask. The best way isn't to frame it as a request for praise or criticism. You could use my **Million-Dollar Question**—a query with a great potential payoff.

It's valuable because it:

- Is focused on the employee more than you;
- Is easy for employees to answer without feeling they must provide a major evaluation;
- Carries with it an assumption that you have the power—and the desire—to help;
- Can be asked in the course of routine interactions;
- Is specific and action-oriented.

Here it is:

Is there anything you need more of—or less of—from me?

Try it. You'll find it can lead to great insights from staff. Some will be about the organization—everything from "I really could use more advance notice on schedule changes" to "I wish we could have fewer meetings that end without a plan." And some will focus on you: "Honestly, I wish I could get more of your full attention when I'm talking with you," or "Sometimes you seem angry when someone questions your idea. It would be nice to have less of that." The personal answers come forward when people believe you are the Truly Interested Boss, not that person's Evil Twin: the Boss Who Read an Advice Book and Is Just Going Through the Motions.

Most of all listen, really listen to what they say and work like the devil to act on it. That's something Evil Twins would never do.

CHECK YOURSELF

Here's another way to determine the trust you've built as a manager and whether you're already on your way to becoming a great boss. Take this "Great Boss Impact" assessment. I'll make it easy. No grades on this one. Here's hoping you can reply to each question with an unqualified yes. But if not, don't despair. There's plenty of help in the chapters ahead.

CHECK YOURSELF: ASSESS YOUR IMPACT

1. Do people come to you regularly and frequently with ideas or projects they're developing rather than wait for instructions or permission? *If they do, it's a good sign they don't feel micromanaged. They feel free to get started on things because you've been clear on roles, responsibilities, expectations, and budgets.*

2. Do people offer their opinions freely in conversations and meetings, without waiting to hear what you think? *People who feel overly controlled or criticized, or believe their opinions don't matter, often shut down. It's safer for them to wait to hear what the boss wants before speaking.*

3. Do your employees tell you about people who'd be great potential employees? *One of the best signs that people like their jobs is their willingness to recommend*

(Continued)

other good people, especially those they know. They're endorsing the workplace and its leadership.

4. Do your staff members talk to you in terms of the whole organization, not just their group's work? *If they do, it is a sign that you've helped them share a vision for the whole organization, and with your leadership they're working as a team, not a silo. (More on that in chapter 12.)*

5. Do your people admit mistakes or misgivings to you? *When your staff is forthcoming with you about errors, it shows you've built a culture of trust and accountability. There's more FYI than CYA. There's more "speaking truth to power" because people see you as approachable, even when the news isn't great.*

6. Do the people you supervise ask you for help AFTER they've tried to solve problems or conflicts among themselves? *If so, you've established a work environment where people don't succeed by lobbying behind one another's backs, nor by turning to you to resolve conflicts before they have given it their best effort. You're a leader, not a parent.*

7. Do you hear your staff talking about values, and if so, do they speak of them as their own, not yours? *It might be ego-boosting to hear people say, "What would the boss do in a case like this?" But what you really want is for people to have a shared sense of values. You might actually hear them discussing a tough call and be proud of the process they use to make a decision on their own.*

8. Do you know your staff members as people, not just producers? Do you know what they hold dear outside of work? *Great bosses know that leadership is professional and personal.*

9. Can you look at your team and see your potential replacement? *The best bosses hire people who are smarter than they are. They aren't intimidated by the strengths and skills of staffers, and they recognize the importance of grooming others to lead.*

10. Could you ask your staff to answer these questions and be pleased with the results? *May I suggest you give it a try? But if you're an aspiring great boss, you've already thought of that.*

It takes power to make an impact like this in the workplace. Do you have enough of the right kind? Let's find out.

CHAPTER 3

How to Tap the Power Grid
of Leadership

I looked out at the professional women I was addressing at a luncheon and asked them to help me with an icebreaker exercise. Would they kindly introduce themselves to the others seated at their tables, using the following words:

"Hello. I am a power-hungry woman."

The room erupted into laughter as hundreds of voices announced their identities as well as that edgy-sounding ambition. When the buzz quieted down, I talked about their response. What is it, I asked, that makes us laugh when we're asked to make such a candid claim? I believe we're demonstrating our discomfort at the thought of publicly coveting clout.

After all, when we call others "power hungry," it's rarely meant as a compliment. It can suggest selfishness, even ruthlessness. It's okay for us to *have* power, but for heaven's sake, we shouldn't appear to be striving for it. It's why many women—and men, too—prefer to have power somehow bestowed on them rather than to actively, openly go for it.

Stanford University business professor Jeffrey Pfeffer is blunt about that challenge in his book *Power: Why Some People Have It—and Others Don't*. He writes:

> Having taught material on power for decades, I have come to believe that the biggest single effect I can have is to get people to *try to become more powerful*. That's because people are afraid of setbacks and the implications for their self-image, so they don't do all they can to increase their power.

Amen. So, repeat after me: "I am a power-hungry boss."

Now, stop chuckling and let's get to work. I'm encouraging you to seek power because you deserve it and you won't succeed without it. In fact, I believe that when you have responsibility but no authority, you've discovered the definition of Managerial Hell. If you've had to work that way, you know what a devil of a time you have. You're held accountable for results but lack the complete set of tools to do the job. With power, you can get things done more effectively, provided you are smart and strategic in how you use it.

I propose that you think in terms of a **power grid**, just like those high-tension towers and wires that energize our daily lives. But managers tap what I call the **Power Grid of Leadership** for the juice that fuels their responsibilities and ambitions.

Now, this particular grid is a little complicated. There are five different sources of power on it, and you have to understand the strengths of each before selecting and tapping into them. I didn't invent these five. They were first identified by social psychologists John French and Bertram Raven back in the 1950s—but I believe they remain completely relevant today. There are five types of power on the grid:

- **Legitimate power**
- **Expert power**
- **Coercive power**
- **Reward power**
- **Referent power**

Let me translate those terms into everyday language and explain what each one means to you as a boss:

Legitimate Power Is Your "Stripes"

It's your title and your rank in the organization. It distinguishes you as someone who has achieved some status and carries some clout. When necessary, you may be able to accomplish things by issuing a mandate. Your vote can trump others. Yours can be the last word.

Some managers assume that legitimate power can supercharge their success. They place a lot of importance on making certain their title brands them as a boss and think people will respond positively to them based on their status. But here's the interesting twist on that. Whenever I want to get a chuckle in a room full of supervisors, I'll say, "Think back to when you moved into management. You thought, 'Now that I have a title I can get things done. People will automatically do what I want.'" Then I ask, "How did that work out?" They laugh, and tell stories about how quickly they learned that titles are ego-boosting and helpful, but that it takes much more than that to accomplish one's goals as a manager. That's especially the case if one of those goals is to be known as a great boss.

Your legitimate power—those stripes on your sleeve— enable you to say, "Do it because I said so!" whenever you choose. But tap that form of power too often and it will backfire. If you feel the need to constantly remind employees that you are in charge, they will probably wish you weren't. They may do what you ask, but they're saluting the uniform, not the person wearing it.

EXPERT POWER IS YOUR "SMARTS"

This is the knowledge you bring to your role. People are often promoted to management because of their demonstrated expertise about the industry, a product, or a process for making things happen. Your expert power might come from deep experience, specialized training, or awards. It could be an innate talent in solving problems for others. Your expertise causes others to turn to you for ideas, resources, and often outright direction. ("You're the master at this, what should we do?") They may accept your guidance without question.

Knowledge is, in fact, power. People want to work for smart bosses. But you need to be wise, too. Wise bosses know that the Evil Twin of "expert" can be "know-it-all" or "micromanager." They don't try to be the smartest person in every facet of the work because they know that's impossible. They aren't afraid to say, "I don't know. What do you think?" They go out of their way to hire employees with expertise they lack and aren't intimidated by employees whose expertise supersedes their own.

They also know the danger of overreliance on their expert power. It may be flattering to have your staff routinely ask, "What would the boss do in a case like this?"—but if that's all they do, they aren't building the critical thinking skills that enable them to innovate and problem-solve on their own.

COERCIVE POWER IS YOUR "STICK"

It's your ability to threaten and to follow through on your threats with punishment. It may seem like one of the most highly charged forms of power on the grid—and guaranteed to drive a response. It is, in fact, an important resource for managers. But you must wield it at the right time, for the right reasons, and with just the right amount of force.

Go ahead and swing that stick when you're dealing with serious malfeasance. Tap into your coercive power when you must warn someone about the consequences of repeated poor performance or sanction those who do serious harm. Punch a bully in the nose—metaphorically speaking, that is. (We'll deal with how to have those tough conversations in chapter 10.) But be strategic. Recognize that fear is a potent force that can deliver short-term results in specific situations, but can burn you if it's the only type of power you rely on.

Stanford business professor Robert Sutton has paid special attention to the misuse of coercive power among bosses. In his book *Good Boss, Bad Boss*, he writes about "bossholes." (Yes, the compound term incorporates the word you think it does.) He cites research that says employees with abusive bosses are more likely to slow down or make intentional errors, hide from bosses, not give maximum effort, and take sick time when they're not really sick.

Simply put, people respect bosses who use their coercive power judiciously. But they don't do their best work in a climate of anxiety, and rarely choose to follow bosses who specialize in scaring them.

REWARD POWER IS YOUR "SWEETS"

This is your capacity to provide something of value in exchange for performance. Like coercion, rewards can seem to be strong sources of power. Who wouldn't want to perform for prizes, right? Well, it's not as simple as that. Few people will turn down a perk, a bonus, or an award, but it doesn't mean they necessarily hold you, the boss, in high regard just because you dispense those goodies. As the Beatles aptly put it, "Money can't buy me love"—and believe it or not, it doesn't necessarily buy motivation from employees. We'll look closely at that in chapter 8 when we drill down on motivation.

This news may actually come as a relief to bosses in these days of tighter budgets and fewer benefits to distribute. I'm not saying you should ignore rewards as a source of power from the grid. Just don't assume you're destined for success if you can dole out the sweets. The challenge for leaders is to understand what is of genuine value to each employee and how to deliver rewards in ways that are practical, sustainable, and meaningful.

Referent Power Is Your "Substance"

I must admit that I had never encountered the term "referent power" until I read French and Raven's work, and "referent" isn't a word I drop into everyday conversation. It might sound clunky, but it's the meaning that matters. And it matters. At its best, referent power is like respect on steroids. When you have referent power, people identify with you and what you stand for. They believe you walk your talk and they aspire to be like you.

The word "charismatic" is sometimes associated with this description, but great bosses who tap the referent source on the power grid are more than charming or cool. The intellect and integrity they bring to their interactions actually causes others to feel more confident, competent, and committed when they're on the same team.

To show you the impact of referent power in the real world, let me reach again into my collection of 360-degree feedback given to managers. Take a look at what three colleagues wrote about one highly regarded boss:

He has qualities such as courage, confidence, innovation, creativity, wisdom, and commitment. He has our trust and respect.

He makes people feel special. They are ready to climb big mountains for him when he asks them to.

Even though he is under enormous pressure, he is always fun and encouraging. He surrounds himself with people who have the same drive. You can easily get high from working with him.

Wow. Who knew a boss could be intoxicating? Referent power sounds mighty potent, doesn't it? Develop it, and it can supercharge your "stripes," enhance your "smarts," intensify your "sweets," and even justify your "stick" when circumstances call for it. Notice that I said "develop" it. Like the power that comes from expertise, referent power is something you earn by hard work and study: the kind you'll do right now.

It's time for a quiz.

Let's return to the power grid for a sense of how *you* tap into each of the five types.

I've taken each source of power and listed five statements under each. I'd like you to indicate your reaction—whether you think the statement is true, false, or you're just not sure right now. It's okay to be unsure. Some of the questions are a bit challenging and there's lots of learning ahead. The goal of this exercise is to check your current knowledge and assumptions about power—and to help you identify your potential to become stronger and smarter about tapping it.

CHECK YOURSELF: TAPPING THE POWER GRID OF LEADERSHIP

Below are a series of statements about the five sources of power. Read each and indicate your agreement or disagreement by writing "True" or "False" next to each statement. If you're not sure, write "NS." Check your responses against the answers and explanations in each section. When you are finished, add up your scores from each section for a total score.

Legitimate:

1. A title can increase a manager's ability to get things done. _____

2. The organization's chain of command should always be respected. _____

3. Rank has its privileges, and should. _____

4. People may or may not like bosses, but should respect them. _____

5. Managers shouldn't hesitate to "play the boss card" to get results. _____

Legitimate—Answers and Explanations:

1. **True.** Titles don't make you a better boss, but there are people inside and outside the organization who respond positively to people based on status.

(Continued)

2. **False.** The tricky word here is "always." Chain of command is usually worth following, but bosses who are rigid about it may stifle communication, collaboration, and candor.

3. **True.** But only when the privileges are reasonable and commensurate with responsibilities: expense accounts, scheduling flexibility, and access to technology. But effective bosses don't flaunt or abuse their privileges.

4. **True.** Employees in organizations are expected to treat managers with respect. But it's up to the boss to earn respect as a person, not just a titleholder.

5. **False.** You *should* hesitate to invoke the "do it because I'm the boss" card. If you use it too frequently, you are forcing people rather than leading them. It's a sign of staff problems, leadership problems, or both.

Number of correct responses: _____

Expert:

1. If people say, "I hope to someday know as much as you," bosses should feel honored. _____

2. Past professional experience and accomplishments guarantee a person's success as a manager. _____

3. Managers should be among the smartest people in the organization. _____

4. Skilled bosses should frequently tell employees, "Here's how I'd do it." _____

5. Bosses should sometimes roll up their sleeves and join the frontline work; it shows people they can produce the quality they expect from others. _____

Expert—Answers and Explanations:

1. **True.** Genuine feedback like that is a tribute to your knowledge. At the same time, you should be equally delighted—not threatened—when your employees build their own expertise.

2. **False.** Experience and accomplishments as an employee are valuable, but they don't guarantee success as a manager. Managing others takes an entirely new set of skills.

3. **True.** Managers should be among the smartest people in the organization—smart enough to hire other very smart people and smart enough to admit what they don't know.

4. **False.** If bosses frequently talk about their personal way of doing things, they can be perceived as egocentric and controlling—and fail to help their staff develop their own solutions.

(Continued)

5. **True.** But only if you do it sometimes, when people need and appreciate your help, and not to show off or micromanage.

   Number of correct responses _____

Coercive:

1. Bosses who are kindhearted are routinely taken advantage of. _____

2. Bosses can be tough, as long as they are tough but fair. _____

3. Managers should always push back when challenged, or they'll be seen as weak and lose respect. _____

4. Bosses who avoid conflict cause problems for the organization. _____

5. Machiavelli was on target when he wrote in *The Prince* that "it is much safer to be feared than loved." _____

Coercive—Answers and Explanations:

1. **False.** Don't assume kindhearted bosses are so soft that they're routinely manipulated. It's possible to be kind and still hold people accountable.

2. **True.** Tough bosses aren't necessarily bullies, provided they respect human dignity, treat people fairly, and know when to lighten up.

3. **False.** Smart bosses don't see every challenge as a threat to their power. They're willing to listen to criticism, admit when they're wrong—and also when to fight the good fight.

4. **True.** Conflict doesn't get better when bosses avoid dealing with it.

5. **False.** Sorry, Machiavelli fans, it's not the 1500s, workplaces aren't kingdoms, and leaders don't ensure their power by sheer intimidation. Don't assume you have to choose between love and fear. Earn both for all the right reasons.

Number of correct responses: _____

Reward:

1. Generosity is an important attribute of a good boss.
   _____

2. Money is the primary motivator for most people.
   _____

3. Managers should provide frequent praise and positive reinforcement for their employees. _____

4. When companies don't provide a budget for perks and gifts, managers have a much harder time getting respect and performance from employees.
   _____

(Continued)

5. When salaries and overtime are frozen or cut, employees lose respect for their immediate supervisors. _____

Reward—Answers and Explanations:

1. **True.** Great bosses are generous about rewarding performance—not just with money, but with things that cost little or nothing: listening, mentoring, feedback, humor, opportunities to learn and grow.

2. **False.** Money is only one of many motivators. Many employees leave good-paying jobs because they lack other important qualities that bosses fail to provide.

3. **True.** Don't be stingy with praise and positive feedback. They matter most when they are sincere and specific.

4. **False.** Perks and gifts are a nice benefit, but bosses who don't have budgets for them can still achieve results and respect.

5. **False.** No one expects employees to be happy about salary or benefit cuts, but their dissatisfaction is usually directed at their company's leadership, not the immediate supervisors they respect.

Number of correct responses: _____

Referent:

1. It is important for leaders to share their vision and values. _____

2. Bosses can build a powerful mystique by keeping aloof from employees. _____

3. Leaders can be realistic and idealistic at the same time. _____

4. It is easier for a boss to build referent power when business is good. _____

5. Leaders at any level of an organization can provide inspiration to the staff. _____

Referent—Answers and Explanations:

1. **True.** Don't fear that talking about a vision or values is corny or "touchy-feely." In fact, it can be motivating to a team and build referent power in a leader.

2. **False.** "Mystique" relates to mystery, rather than the authenticity of referent power, and keeping a distance from employees can build mistrust.

3. **True.** Realism and idealism aren't incompatible. Great bosses communicate both—and add optimism to boot.

4. **False.** Challenging times, when people need encouragement and energy, can be the crucible of referent power. Bad times can produce great leaders.

(Continued)

5. **True.** Referent power is not reserved for managers. Anyone in the organization can earn it.

Number of correct responses: _____

TOTAL CORRECT ANSWERS: _____

CHECK YOURSELF: MAKING SENSE OF YOUR RESPONSES

Now that you've tallied your answers, I suggest you take a look at key questions:

1. **What was your total number of correct replies?** If you scored more than 20, I say "more power to you!" You understand strategic approaches to tapping the grid—and I suspect you are acting on them already. If you had fewer than 20 correct, don't despair. Some of my questions were tricky and required nuanced answers. Understanding those nuances is key to becoming a great boss, and I'll provide lots of help in the chapters ahead.

2. **In which of the power sources did you have the most—and the fewest—correct answers?** What do you think it means about your relationship with those specific sources of power? What assumptions or beliefs might I have challenged? What did your answers reveal about how you think great bosses behave? What does this leave you hungry to learn more about?

Here's a suggestion: After you finish taking in the full scope of information in this book, go back and take the quiz again. I know you'll raise your score. Let me also suggest that this quiz could also be a great group exercise for a leadership team. Compare your answers and ideas, and discuss how you can work together to earn and share power.

While we're focusing on power, it's the perfect time to ask you an important question:

Are You a Manager, a Leader, or Both?

You've probably noticed that I've been using the words "boss," "supervisor," "manager," and "leader" in describing your rank, your role, and your responsibilities. Some would argue that I shouldn't commingle the word "leader" with the others because leadership is a special class all its own.

It's an interesting argument—one that often takes place in business school classes. Let's take it on, and make it personal. What do you think? Do you consider yourself a manager, a leader, or both? And how do you define each? I suspect your answer may be, "I don't know, I've been too busy working to give it much thought." And I would understand.

So let's turn to social scientists who have devoted large chunks of their brainpower and working lives to defining and differentiating the concepts of management and leadership. Check out the box below. It's the perspectives of two top leadership scholars, John Kotter of Harvard and Warren Bennis of the University of Southern California, distilled into a snapshot:

	The Manager	**The Leader**
John Kotter	Copes with complexity Plans and budgets Organizes and staffs Controls and problem-solves	Copes with change Sets a direction Aligns people Motivates people
Warren Bennis	Promotes efficiency Is a good soldier Imitates Accepts the status quo Does things right	Promotes effectiveness Is his or her own person Originates Challenges Does the right things

Sources: John P. Kotter, "What Leaders Really Do," Harvard Business Review, *May-June 1990. Warren Bennis and Joan Goldsmith,* Learning to Lead: A Workbook on Becoming a Leader *(New York: Basic Books, 2003).*

It's pretty clear that they are describing managers as front-line "doers," and leaders as being focused on bigger-picture issues. But I'm concerned that those definitions are too limiting. I worry most that you could be tempted to see managers as lesser beings than leaders, drudges who feed the machine while leaders create visions of a better world.

So let me call on one more leadership scholar, Joseph C. Rost. He's written, "Any concept of leadership that dignifies leadership at the expense of management has to be defective." He praises effective managers for bringing order, stability, organization, and goal achievement to the workplace.

Rost is absolutely right. Employees appreciate managers who keep the trains running on time, because they know it's hard work. They also know that effective managers remove obstacles to employee success. Take a look at a feedback quote for a manager who really fits that description. The employee wrote this about her:

Very organized. She has a scheduling computer hot-wired into her brain. Good at delegating what needs delegating. Quick to develop new approaches to streamline processes. Doesn't waste her time or others. Alert, aware, and accommodating.

You can tell from the economy of words in that message that this is an employee who really values efficiency—and the boss more than delivers. That's impressive management.

So let's hear it for managers and let's not think of them as almost-as-good-as-leaders.

Because the truth is that you can be a wonderful manager without being a leader. You can also be a leader without ever being a manager. You can also be both. As Rost aptly puts it, management is about **authority**, and leadership is about **influence**.

That, I believe, is the clear and critical distinction. Managers have the authority to make things happen. They can do it by tapping the grid for a shot of reward or coercive power, or try a zap of legitimate power by simply pulling rank. That's **authority**.

But managers who are also leaders—and leaders who aren't managers—have something in common. They achieve their goals through **influence**.

Influence comes from trust and respect. And my goodness, doesn't it sound like you are back at the grid tapping that old referent power? You are. Influence isn't necessarily related to titles and rank. I often ask managers in my seminars to tell me about people in their organizations who have no formal titles at all but are clearly seen as leaders. Inevitably, I hear about people who have strong credibility with colleagues, not only for what they know, but for their very apparent values and how they live them. They are people whose opinions hold more weight, whose praise means a great deal to others, and who, when they suggest a course of action, are likely to see people step up to comply.

So now that you have a pretty good handle on the whole management/leadership thing, how can you tell if *you* are a manager with authority, a leader with influence—or both?

My answer is simple. You don't determine that; your colleagues do. In the end, it all comes down to this:

- People are **required** to follow managers.
- People **choose** to follow leaders.

Should you strive to be both manager and leader? Absolutely. It's why all of my workshops, teaching, and writing are about both. One supports the other, especially in these times of flatter organizations. You may find yourself working on projects in which you aren't the boss of everyone involved—and your best route to results is your influence as a leader.

So, would you please repeat after me:

"Hello, I'm a power-hungry manager and an influence-hungry leader."

There, you said it. Good for you. Good for your employees, too, who stand to benefit from that declaration. But there's lots of work to do to make certain you live up to those words.

So, let's explore how to manage the most challenging person on your team: *you.*

CHAPTER 4

Manage Yourself, So You Can Lead Others

It's not a sexy word. Not dynamic. Frankly, it sounds more boring than inspiring. But when spoken about bosses, it is priceless. The simple word is:

Calm. As in "calm in the storm."

I noticed that word appearing more often in feedback about managers shortly after the horrors of September 11, 2001. That shared time of crisis seemed to raise the profile and value of coolheadedness. In seminars, we'd ask our traditional open-ended feedback question about bosses: "When it comes to leadership and management, what are this person's strengths?" Now that simple word, "calm," was surfacing commonly as a compliment. As survey researchers will tell you, when a word appears in responses frequently and unprompted, you ought to pay attention to it. I did, still do, and so should you.

Why get excited about "calm in the storm" as a managerial aptitude? Because tough times reveal the best and the worst in people. When you're in charge, your professional reputation can be made or broken by your grace under pressure.

Think of Captain Chesley "Sully" Sullenberger, the veteran pilot who finessed his disabled US Airways plane to a safe landing on the icy Hudson River in January 2009, saving all 155 souls on board. His technical execution was breathtaking. The event was dubbed "the Miracle on the Hudson."

But while others celebrated Sullenberger's stellar aeronautic prowess, I was deeply impressed by his top-flight leadership qualities. Here's what I admired:

- He consistently broadened the spotlight beyond himself. In every public appearance and interview, he took pains to share credit with the other professionals on his team.
- He resisted the mantle of "hero," preferring instead to attribute his stellar performance to a lifelong focus on rigorous training, systems, practice, and standards.
- He emphasized values; Sullenberger's book about the event could have been titled with words like "terror" or "miracle" to grab attention and ring up sales. Instead, his choice was *Highest Duty: My Search for What Really Matters.*

One thing that clearly matters to Captain Sully is the leader's responsibility to have—and to project—a sense of calm in crisis. He said this in a magazine article:

> It wasn't until about 90 seconds before we hit the water that I spoke to the passengers. I wanted to be very direct. I didn't want to sound agitated or alarmed. I wanted to sound professional. "This is the captain. Brace for impact!"

Think about that. At a time when every millisecond mattered and this man's every brain cell needed to focus on a precise sequence of actions, the captain was mindful of the tone of his voice and the choice of his words. He understood what great leaders and great bosses know: Emotions matter, and they are contagious.

Most managers won't find themselves in Sullenberger's life-and-death situation, but they do face pressure, deadline, conflict, and the occasional crisis. Some respond poorly; they may shut down or blow up, may be indecisive or rash, may cause panic, confusion, and errors.

Inept managers magnify our stress. The best ones relieve it, while still achieving the organization's goals. They sense what people need in good times and in bad—and deliver. When they do, they get feedback like this:

> *Her interpersonal skills are peerless. You can always rely upon her to "keep her head about her when all others are losing theirs." Her cheerful demeanor is contagious and has a calming effect on the room, where deadline pressures can often lead to short tempers.*

GETTING SMART ABOUT EMOTIONAL INTELLIGENCE

The ability to size up a situation and consciously, strategically select the best response is a key part of what's called **emotional intelligence**. It is a relatively young field of study, one that only recently has been recognized as an important managerial aptitude. And even today, emotional intelligence (often referred to as "EI" or "EQ") is referred to as a boss's "soft skills." Soft? I fear that in the rough-and-tumble world of work, that term might sound kind of wimpy. But trust me, those soft skills of yours can produce a rock-solid payback.

Take it from Harvard business school professor Linda A. Hill. She says that twenty years ago, the MBA students in her university's hallowed halls weren't inclined to view emotional intelligence as part of the path to business success. How times have changed! In her book *Becoming a Manager,* she says that these days, "They walk around talking about their 'EQ,' and our alumni report to us that it is the 'soft stuff' that differentiates the winners from the losers."

Let's make sure you're among the winners, by helping you understand some hard facts about soft skills. First of all, don't assume emotional intelligence is a fancy way of repackaging what your parents taught you about being nice, polite, or kind. It's far more.

A pioneer researcher in the field, psychologist John Mayer, describes EI this way: *The ability to accurately perceive your own and other's emotions; to understand the signals that emotions send about relationships; and to manage your own and others' emotions.*

Let's get even more specific, and break things down to

four distinct areas of EI skills. They come from the work of psychologist Daniel Goleman. He worked as a science writer for the *New York Times* in the '80s and '90s, and became fascinated by EI and its impact. He left the *Times* to dive more deeply into the study of emotional intelligence, becoming its best-known evangelist. I often recommend his book *Primal Leadership*, in which he outlines these four EI "domains":

- **Self-awareness** (How well you know yourself)
- **Self-management** (How well you regulate yourself)
- **Social awareness** (Your ability to see things through the eyes of others)
- **Relationship management** (Your interpersonal skills)

Goleman and others believe that managers with intelligence, professional expertise, and business savvy boost their effectiveness by mastering emotional intelligence, and may sabotage their own success if they lack it. From my experience with thousands of managers, I agree. In fact, I think EI is often the Achilles' heel of otherwise smart bosses. They are managers who are better with products and process than with people.

Managers lacking in EI tap only three sources of power on our famous grid: **legitimate** ("Do it because I said so"), **expert** ("Do it my way because I know best"), and **coercive** ("Do it or there will be hell to pay"). They neglect the two that have the most interpersonal impact: **reward** ("I know we're going to be celebrating your success") and **referent** ("This is work that really matters and you're a key part of it"). They fail to build positive relationships and undercut their opportunities to build influence. Their lack of people skills ultimately holds them back.

I recall a very sharp and charming manager whose eyes were really opened by the feedback she received in one of my management seminars. She was justifiably proud of her commitment to quality and her genuine passion for her profession. But while her self-image was "Passionate Boss," she clearly had an Evil Twin, "Pit Bull." In her feedback, a colleague clearly gave her credit for her talent, then deftly delivered the bad news. He told her she had every tool to be successful. However...

Beware not to show verbally aggressive behavior and argue with colleagues when there is no need to. Not every detail is important. Even though you mean no harm in the way you talk to people, not everyone knows that behind your harsh language and tone, there is an absolutely wonderful, nice, and very, very skillful colleague.

I give great credit to the person who wrote that feedback, because its content and tone demonstrated emotional intelligence. Knowing this manager well, he selected the right balance of candor and care to nudge rather than kick her toward change. Though initially bruised by the bad news, she heeded the wake-up call. I helped her develop a plan to channel her passion in more constructive ways—and build (or repair) bridges to her staff.

If you want to be a great boss, you're not going to get there without emotional intelligence. But how do you know if yours is weak or well developed? Let's run through the all-important competencies and I'll ask you some questions to help you assess your EI.

Check Yourself: EI, EI, Oh?

Self-Awareness

Do you have a good handle on your own strengths and weaknesses?

Some people are much better than others at identifying where they excel, do fairly well, or need work. If you're the boss, people may be reluctant to critique you (at least to your face). That puts an extra responsibility on you to not only seek out feedback (see the Million-Dollar Question in chapter 2) and do your best to inventory your skill set. In addition to being aware of your strong points and shortcomings, it's important to understand the effect they have on other people. If, for example, your weaknesses include a short fuse or short attention span, long-windedness or long attachments to old grudges, then what's all that doing to other people who look to you for leadership? How are you making their lives more difficult?

Are you able to read your own emotions?

If you're having an "up" or "down" day, do you recognize it? Are you able to figure out exactly what emotions are in play, for better or worse—and why? Are you aware of how you project—or don't project—the emotions you experience? Are you seen as an optimist or a pessimist? Do people tell you that you are easy to read and mean it as a compliment—or say you are hard to read and mean it as a concern?

*Do you know if, how, and when your emotions
enhance or hijack your thinking?*

Do you find yourself making bad decisions when you are
tired or stressed? (Science, by the way, says it's likely.) Do
you say things in the heat of the moment that, on reflection,
you regret? Worse yet, do you say things in the heat of the
moment and not reflect on them at all, only to discover that
you've done damage? Do your emotional reactions to certain
people and situations cause you to shut down, make poor
snap judgments, or develop biases? If you're delighted by flattery or depressed by a hard-luck story, are you less likely to
rely on logic and reason in your decision-making?

Self-Management

*If you are aware of your strengths and weaknesses,
do you do something about them?*

Sad to say, there are people who don't attempt to get past the
self-awareness stage. A colleague of mine shares a story that
perfectly illustrates this. During college, he worked in construction as a laborer. Here's how he describes his foreman:
"The immortal words of my boss, used most often immediately following some irrational decision or demand, were,
'That's just me. I'm an asshole. Always have been, always
will be.'"

As my friend points out, that boss was amazingly self-
aware—and definitely *not* self-managing. He wore the mantle
of his mismanagement proudly, and rather than do something
about it, he expected others to adapt. I may have told you that

rank does indeed carry some privileges, but exempting yourself from self-management isn't one of them. If you're short-tempered, you master cool-down techniques. If you have a great need to be liked, you get training in how to tackle tough conversations. In short, you hold yourself accountable for your own improvement and actively work on it.

Can you adapt to change and challenges?

Are you known for being able to roll with the punches? Do you make it your business to keep cool under pressure? Are you a glass-half-full person? Do you display a sense of optimism even when others are getting discouraged? Emotional resilience is a hallmark of emotional intelligence. I think it also relates directly to that referent power we talked about earlier. People choose to follow leaders who shine like a beacon in dark times. But a positive outlook isn't just an antidote to gloom. Optimists believe that good things are more likely to happen than bad. When you have it and share it, you're encouraging people toward making changes and trying new things, and discouraging them from giving up prematurely. As a bonus, research has even linked optimism to better health. So clearly, your optimism can make even a sunny day brighter.

Do you know if, why, and how your words and actions inspire trust in others?

Self-managing bosses build what's called "social capital." It's your bank account of trust and goodwill, something that carries you through those times when your decisions inevitably disappoint people. It means you actively work to build trust—you don't assume people owe it to you because you're in charge. You take pains to make certain it's you—and not your

Evil Twin—who's in the room at any time. You are mindful of those things that employees never forget and never forgive—and consciously work to do the right thing. In short, you manage yourself so you can lead others.

Social Awareness

Do you have the ability to read the emotions of others?

Can you accurately assess how people are feeling based on their facial expressions or body language? Can you discern nervous laughter from a genuine guffaw? Can you tell when a person is apprehensive, defensive, or offended? Are you quick to notice when someone isn't his or her normal self? Can you sense when your words just aren't connecting with someone, and shift to a different approach? And if, like one manager I coached, social awareness isn't your strong suit, do you strive to bridge that gap? I really admired his sincere acknowledgment that he missed the social cues others noticed, and he worked hard to improve. If that sounds like you, it's important to enlist allies who can help you see what you're overlooking.

Do you know how to "read the room"?

Can you walk into a workspace or a meeting room and easily take the temperature of the team? Can you sense whether they're energized, demoralized, or distracted—and respond accordingly? My personal philosophy as a manager was, "My job is to be calm if everyone is nervous, and get nervous if they're all too calm." In a 24/7 world of breaking news, the demand for both speed and accuracy creates great pressure on people and performance. I'm sure I was no Captain Sully, but I believed that the greater the stress level during any given event, the more I had to respond with calm confidence—to set the tone for the team. Conversely, if I'd sensed we were getting a little complacent, I'd add energy and urgency to the way I talked—and even walked.

Do you demonstrate genuine empathy?

Let's be clear about the term. Empathy isn't the sentiment you express *about* someone's situation ("I'm happy for you," or "Please accept my sincere condolences")—that's sympathy, and its valuable. But you can be sympathetic without ever knowing a person. Empathy is far more powerful. It is the ability to see the world through someone else's eyes. It takes a good deal more work to step out of your own frame of reference and into someone else's shoes. You can't do that from a distance. It requires that you hone your listening skills and be able to reflect back to the other person not just what they said, but your understanding of what they meant. Like leadership, the best assessment of your empathy doesn't come from you. There's a big difference between your saying, "I know how you feel," and having the other person believe that you do. When people sense that you're open to seeing the world through their eyes, it builds trust.

Relationship Management

Do you provide feedback, guidance, and inspiration to others?

Some of the best supervisors I know measure their personal success by the accomplishments of others. They make it a priority not to simply get good work out of employees, but to play a direct role in helping them grow—and soar. They get to know their staff as people, not just producers. They serve as coaches, mentors—and even role models. One of the first columns I ever wrote for managers stressed the importance of this, and I chose a title to drive the point home. It was "I'm Your Leader, What Have I Done for You Lately?" You need to work for them, not just assume they work for you. If you think you simply don't have time enough in the day for this kind of personal interaction, or if you assume it's not really part of your job, you are missing an opportunity to become a great boss.

Do you build bonds with people, foster teamwork, and network effectively?

You might have great relationships with your immediate staff, but what about those who work elsewhere in the organization? Do you go out of your way to make meaningful connections, and to encourage your employees to do the same? How's your "balance of trade" with people in other departments, doing other jobs? Do you interact with them only when you need something from them and ignore them the rest of the time? Do you respond to their needs with the same generosity and speed you expect from them? And let me ask a very specific and telling question: How well do you know the people who clean your workplace? Do you know their names, anything about their families, or what's important to them in the work they do? Emotionally intelligent people tend to be among the best at recognizing and respecting the people behind all sorts of jobs. They don't know "Maintenance Guy," "HR Lady," or "IT Dude"—they know Roy, Nico, and Jeff.

Do you share a vision that people can see and want to be part of?

Let's say you're the boss of Roy, Nico, or Jeff. Though I'd like to assume you talk with them about your vision for the work they do, I know that in many organizations it doesn't happen. Or if it does, it might sound something like this:

> **ROY,** we're not paid to think, we're paid to clean up for people who think they do.
>
> **NICO,** we're forever juggling people and their paperwork. Our job is make sure our records are perfect so we don't get sued.
>
> **JEFF,** don't let them take too much of your time, we can't keep the systems running if we're always holding someone's hand.

Do you see any vision there? I don't. And I'm sure our mythical employees aren't particular inspired by those words. Does that matter? Absolutely. So:

> **ROY,** because of us, this is a welcoming place for visitors, and one of the most environmentally conscious buildings in the area.
>
> **NICO,** people here depend on us to do what's right for them through good times and bad. We're the quiet giant when it comes to employee engagement.
>
> **JEFF,** now more than ever, this business needs digital leaders and thinkers. We're more than problem-solvers, we're innovators.

Can you see my vision about vision?

YOU ARE A WALKING BILLBOARD, BOSS. WHAT'S YOUR MESSAGE?

As we focus on emotional intelligence, it's time for a reminder about a management fact of life. Bosses, nothing you say or do goes unnoticed. It's true. When you become a supervisor, you're "always on." Someone's always watching you, looking for cues and clues to questions like:

- How are things really going?
- How am I doing, boss?
- What's important to you?

If employees ask you those questions personally, you'd answer them. But this isn't about direct conversations. It's about the way people translate your actions as they observe you.

Knowing you're always on—on stage, on display, open to interpretation—can be intimidating. It can also be empowering, as you learn to be strategic, intentional, and clear in your words and deeds, lest people misread you.

And believe me, they do. I often ask veteran managers, "Have you ever discovered a rule that you never knew you made?" Indeed they have. They tell stories about casual remarks, one-off suggestions, or situations that morphed— without their knowledge—into a mandate attributed to them.

For example, you can be sitting in a meeting and make some offhand comment like, "I'm exchanging text messages with more people these days. You know, I fear those weird abbreviations everyone uses are going to turn us into a world of terrible spellers." Next thing you know, there's a buzz going around the staff: "Don't ever send a message to the boss using an abbreviation."

It's not what you said. It's not what you meant. But it's out there. You are a walking billboard, whether you know it or not. So tune up your self-awareness and social awareness and be on the alert for miscues.

Here are some of the most common "rules you never knew you made" and "messages you never knew you sent" that I encounter in my work with managers and their staffs.

Mistaken Message: Work like me.

People watch the hours you keep. If you're a start early/stay late boss, some staff may assume you expect them to match you, hour for hour. It's common for people to think the way to keep your respect is to be there when you are. Be clear about your expectations. And repeat them often.

Mistaken Message: Talk to me 24/7.

Technology is our friend, but it can telegraph wrong messages. Recently, a manager told me she's changed her habit of sending staff emails very late at night or early in the morning. To her, it was simply about getting tasks done or thoughts captured before she forgot them. But for her staff, the wee-hours time stamp on her emails seemed like pressure to reply ASAP. Today, the manager still writes those moonlight emails, but she files them as drafts and sends them out at reasonable hours.

Mistaken Message: I like these folks best.

Great bosses know that when they work the room (as they should), people are watching and listening. If you spend too much time, too often, commiserating with one group of staff or with certain individuals, they can be seen as your favored few. Recently, a new manager told me he realized he'd been spending way too much time stopping by the small work group he was part of before his promotion. It was his comfort zone. The rest of the staff wanted his attention, yet he was bypassing them on his way to chew the fat with old comrades. His self-awareness led to self-management. He became an equal-opportunity chatter.

Mistaken Message: Here's how people should be treated.

When people see you address the cleaning crew and the CEO with the same level of respect, they can't miss the message about your standards. If you make it a point to visibly network and collaborate with other work groups, rather than just talk about "those people" from afar, your team is less likely to become a silo. If you characterize complaining customers as pests to be exterminated rather than relationships to be elevated, you'll hear echoes of yourself not just in their words, but in their work. After all, you wrote their script.

Mistaken Message: Life is good/bad/so-so.

Is your office door open or closed? Are you walking with your head up or down? Are you smiling more or less these days? Giving more compliments or criticisms? Turns out that you're not only a walking billboard, you're the barometer for the pressure in the workplace, especially in a tough economy or times of change. Now, *you* might not be thinking anything negative at all, but people who are fearful of the worst may read bad news into your behaviors, so beware. And one more warning:

Emotions Are Contagious

I hope I've made a persuasive case for the importance of emotional intelligence and what it looks like in action. But you might be holding out for more, thinking in true business-like fashion: Show me the ROI of EI.

You want return on investment? I think the business case for EI was impressively made in a recent study reported by the Wharton Business School. It's called "Why Does Affect Matter in Organizations?" "Affect" means emotions, moods, and dispositions.

The researchers crunched an array of studies on the role of emotion in organizations and concluded that "the evidence is overwhelming that experiencing and expressing positive emotions and moods tends to enhance performance at individual, group, and organizational levels." They found that emotion has an impact on "performance, decision-making, turnover, pro-social behavior, negotiation, conflict resolution, group dynamics and leadership."

For managers, this is especially important, because the research also shows that *your* emotions are contagious. Yikes! You are now Boss, Billboard, Barometer—and Bacteria!

Seriously, the people who work for you do indeed pick

up on your emotions and your moods. If you are a person who is known to be moody, withdrawn, poker-faced, sarcastic, or testy, your bad vibe is probably going viral. And guess which of your employees are the most likely to want to leave a bummed-out boss and workplace? It's the folks on your staff who are known for their *positive* energy. Their optimism and confidence predispose them to believe that things will be better on another team, so they'll head to those greener pastures. And those chronic complainers and naysayers on your staff, what about them? Their pessimism leads them to assume that things are rotten everywhere, so they'll stay right where they are—with *you*. How's that for ROI?

To lead others, you truly must manage yourself first. And when you do, the payoff can be powerful. You're likely to get feedback as rewarding as this:

> *He is a likable, approachable person. He listens with equal interest to both ideas and complaints. He takes an active role in finding solutions to issues as they arise. He is upbeat and his energy easily spreads to those around him. I feel better and more confident about my job knowing he is at the helm.*

Okay, now it's time for a quick checkup. I'm using a version of an exercise I first introduced when leading a management session at a big convention in Las Vegas. After teaching the key elements of emotional intelligence, I distributed a questionnaire like this one, and asked each person in the room to do a quick self-evaluation.

Would you kindly do the same?

CHECK YOURSELF: HOW HIGH IS YOUR EI?

Please answer the following questions, rating yourself on a scale of 1 to 10, with 10 representing the most positive score, 1 the least positive.

As a boss, to what degree do you believe you are:

1. People-oriented _____

2. Trusted _____

3. Empathetic _____

4. Calm under pressure _____

5. Optimistic _____

6. Aware of—and working on—your weak spots _____

7. Adept at exercising self-control _____

8. Known for networking with others outside your work group _____

9. Skilled at sharing a vision of success _____

10. Inclined to celebrate victories, both big and small _____

Your total score: _____

Now with quizzes like this, you're accustomed to seeing a "What Your Score Means" explanation here. Let's just stipulate that a higher score would, of course, be a good thing, especially if it is accurate. But how do you know it is?

It's time to take you back to Vegas. When everyone in the convention room finished writing, I requested they do something that's usually verboten during conference presentations. Would they kindly take out their cell phones and make some calls?

I asked them to select a couple people back home in their organizations, people whose opinions really matter to them. Call them right now. Read the questionnaire to them and ask for *their* ratings.

Let me pause here and answer your skeptical questions.

- Would bosses really do this? Make cold calls home to ask employees for feedback?
- Upon getting that call out of the blue, would employees tell the truth?

I can only tell you what I witnessed—a yes to both questions. In fact, I wish you could have seen and heard that room, as the long-distance feedback conversations went on for a good ten minutes. I had to drag people off their phones to resume the teaching. When they settled down, I asked what they had discovered during this process. How much similarity did they find between their self-evaluations and their colleagues'? A good number of people discovered that they had truly underrated themselves on several dimensions. For a few others, there was a wake-up call about a blind spot or two.

Many managers said their staffers were surprised to be

asked for feedback from the boss and happy their opinions mattered. I encouraged the managers to keep the conversations going when they returned home from Sin City.

I've done this exercise other times, in other places, with equally positive results. Yes, it's possible that employees pull their punches when the boss asks for feedback. They may be overly diplomatic. But it's always generated useful, actionable feedback for the managers because it sends an amazingly simple and effective message to your staff: You want to listen to them.

So, are you ready to take a gamble? Get our your cell phone, pick some people (employees and coworkers) whose opinions really matter to you—and call. Or better yet, park the phone and talk to them face-to-face.

Speaking of communication...that's our next big lesson.

CHAPTER 5

You and Your Big Mouth: Communication Tips and Traps

The young manager in my seminar was trying, unsuccessfully, to hide her disappointment. She had just read feedback from her staff, fellow managers, and her top boss. I asked what was troubling her. "Look at what my general manager wrote," she replied, shaking her head. While others had provided detailed responses, he'd jotted a one-word reply to each of the questions. The same word, over and over:

"Excellent."

But in this situation, "Excellent" wasn't good enough. Mind you, the recipient wasn't a diva in search of massive ego stroking; she was earnest and down-to-earth. But she was also new to her management job, still trying to figure out her boss, and eager to succeed. She asked me, "How can I get any direction from this? I may be doing things he likes, but what are they?" She wondered if he had even read the questions, and if he had, why he didn't think it worth his time to elaborate.

Meanwhile, it's a safe bet her boss assumed that she'd revel in this report card, never dreaming that his replies—superlative but not substantive—were so disappointing.

That's the kind of disconnect that goes on all the time in organizational communication. I coached that young supervisor on how to dig for more detail from her boss when she got home from our program, to bridge her information gap. But I've never forgotten that lesson in missed opportunity.

DO YOU HAVE "BAD COMMUNICATION BREATH?"

My goal is to help you do what that general manager didn't: to communicate with minimal misunderstanding and maximum impact. You need this more than you may realize. Frankly, when I ask bosses about skills they'd like to master, many will cite things like strategic thinking or budget forecasting or conquering some aspect of technology. They rarely think they need help with communication. It's so common and constant that we take it for granted. It's like *breathing*, right? You just do it. But let's check what's coming out of your mouth, my friend. It just might be "bad communication breath," the kind bosses discover the hard way—if and when they get honest feedback.

Stand back a little. Here's what it smells like:

She many times doesn't allow people to express themselves. She'll jump on their unfinished statements, sometimes incorrectly assuming she knows where they are going. She'll answer questions that are asked of others. She inadvertently creates resentment because colleagues feel she doesn't listen.

Sometimes, I have to make sure that he's paying attention to me if he's looking at the computer while I'm talking to him. I'll ask, "Are you listening to me?"

She uses email when it would be so much easier and definitely more personal (especially when there's bad news) to come to our desks. Her defense of email is this is how she's always communicated. Unfortunately, her emails come across harsher than she does in person.

He needs to improve his communication skills. Important messages often don't get to his staff; they sometimes don't feel clued in or well incorporated into department decision-making. He often doesn't answer messages. It's a source of frustration to his coworkers.

Simply put, that kind of communication stinks. So let's clear the air with some tips you can use the very next time you open your mouth.

FIVE TIPS TO IMMEDIATELY IMPROVE YOUR COMMUNICATION

1. Assume people are hungry for information.

In our personal lives, we are accustomed to having access to information 24/7. We get it in just about any form we want it (print, text, audio, video, instant message, voice mail, email, social media). When we have questions, it's easier than ever to get answers—except at work, and especially from our bosses. Managers are the ultimate gatekeepers, sometimes by design, but often by simple ineptitude. That's not just my observation. The authors of the book *Strategic Organizational Communication in a Global Economy* say:

> One of the most consistent findings in research on organizations is that subordinates want their supervisors to keep them informed and feel that they receive too little relevant and useful information from their supervisors, especially about events, policies and changes directly involving them and their jobs.

So, assume your team members are hungry, underfed, and it's your job to nourish them. But when it comes to communication, don't confuse quantity with quality. (Ask anyone who is buried in email and pointless paperwork.) You need to approach communication strategically. That means you know precisely why, how, and to whom you dispense data on both an ongoing and a situational basis. That's what we'll work on in this chapter.

2. Abandon management-speak.

I hope you've noticed how hard I try to avoid using management buzzwords in this book and to translate research literature into everyday terms. I believe management-speak erodes a leader's credibility. Peppering your messages with terms like "right-size" and "paradigm shift" is the essence of bad communication breath. Nothing says phony like a hard-nosed, bottom-line manager announcing that employees should "embrace change." Embrace? Sounds almost romantic, doesn't it? Like some kind of transition tango. Bosses, just say it plain: *We want employees to understand, accept, adapt, or even master the challenges of change.* Otherwise your people will think you've had a computer chip planted in your head during one too many management retreats.

3. Do a 360-degree stroll around your messages *before* delivering them.

Whenever you're about to distribute important information, take a moment to look in all directions. Think about who else has a stake in the situation you're describing. You may be clear on your intentions and focused on the information's value to your team, but without that 360-degree walk, your communication may come as an unwelcome surprise or unintended slight to other employees. A message of kudos may leave someone out. A reminder about policy may appear to be a public criticism of individuals. A chipper announcement of change may seem callous toward those who are losing something in the process. Smart bosses often run important messages past a trusted coworker or two before hitting SEND or saying, "Could I have your attention, everyone?" That small step can ensure that your words deliver exactly the message you intend—to everyone.

4. Watch your creative language.

Similes, metaphors, and cultural references are powerful rhetorical devices. They can entertain and inspire, especially if they resonate with the interests and values of your staff. But they can also backfire, making you sound clubby or downright clumsy. Some bosses love to refer to the movies, music, and TV shows of their own generation, assuming their experience is universally shared. Some use sports analogies, thinking everyone's a knowledgeable fan. Others use slang or nicknames that can leave people feeling devalued. Who gets to decide if a tech expert is called a "geek" or an accountant a "bean counter"? Even if they use that term for themselves, does it feel the same when managers use it? And don't get me started on loaded gender language like "put on your big girl pants" or "man up." I'm quite happy to "woman up," thank you—have been for some time. Many years ago, in a meeting, I made an announcement to male colleagues who had the habit of describing "courage" by referring to certain male anatomical parts. I said with a smile, "This is a tough decision, but I think we all have the ovaries for it, don't we?" They got the message.

5. Know when to speak in specifics and when in generalities.

As a rule, managers should strive to provide clarity in their messages, and specificity does that. Details, context, next steps—they're all important. But there are some times when ambiguity is actually helpful. A leader may share a vision for a goal and intentionally leave some details open so followers can help design the road map to success. In a brainstorming session, the head of a group might hold off expressing his or her own opinions for a while, so the team won't self-censor or just echo the boss's ideas. When negotiating an important issue or dealing with conflict, there are times when being direct and blunt can shut things down. The authors of the book *The Art of Framing: Mastering the Language of Leadership* say:

> Explicit acknowledgment of a hopeless impasse can end a conversation when ambiguous language might preserve the opening for options not yet discovered. Explicit language assessing blame or fault can cause people to lose face so that they may find it impossible to continue in the relationship.

Managers should weigh the specificity/ambiguity decision with great care, recognizing that too much ambiguity, especially in times of change, can increase fear, rumors, and conflicting interpretations of strategy and tactics. If you feel the need for ambiguity, I suggest you get a second opinion, set a time limit on how long you'll stick with the abstract approach, and begin working on a plan for transitioning to concrete details.

YOUR SECRET WEAPON: OPENING LINES AND CLOSING LOOPS

Let's look at some specific things you can do to add impact to your messages—from start to finish. Remember, as a boss, you are "always on." That's why smart bosses understand the importance of opening lines, both in their casual interactions with people and in their daily work. The first thing you say can set the tone for the rest of your conversations. It can help you develop a reputation for being approachable. It can even telegraph (accurately or inaccurately) what's really important to you.

I saw an interesting illustration of that in the case of a new boss who supervised multiple departments. His staff gave him credit for making needed changes, but some felt his style tended toward micromanagement. In his feedback, an observant staffer suggested that he revisit one of his opening lines. It seems his popular predecessor's first words when encountering staffers had been a genuine "How are you doing?" His differed by only one word: "*What* are you doing?" That might sound like splitting hairs, but people were hearing an Evil Twin message: "I care about the work, not you."

How adept are you at sizing up a situation and choosing those first words of yours with care? Here are four common scenarios. Think about the first words you're most likely to say when:

1. An employee comes to you at a time you are truly busy and asks, "Got a minute?"
2. A staffer hands you a draft of an important report she's written, looking for your feedback.
3. You're leading a brainstorming session.
4. You're calling an employee's home on that person's day off to get some important information.

Everyday exchanges like these bring opportunities to let people know what you stand for—and where they stand with you, right out of the starting gate:

1. **Got a minute?** Instead of waving off the staffer who wants a minute when you have none to give by saying, "Sorry, not now, I'm jammed up," try my favorite reply: "Hi. I have a *minute*, but I bet you deserve more, right? Let's set up a time when I'm out from under this deadline." Note the last sentence, offering an alternative meeting time. You aren't just offering a partial reply. You're doing what's called "closing the loop." More on that in just a bit.

2. **Reviewing the report.** My advice to you comes from years of experience working with writers. The author of just about any piece of work is nervous about how it is going to be accepted. Your opening line can make a world of difference in how they'll accept your suggestions for improvement. Instead of saying, "Let's take a look," and diving into the document to look for holes, start by asking, "What do you love about this report?" or "How can I help?" Opening lines like that establish you as a coach, rather than a corrections officer. Interestingly, they also elicit an almost immediate self-critique from the writer before you even have to mention a weak spot in the report.

3. **Brainstorming.** Many an idea session has sputtered or self-destructed due to the way it was launched. Say you start by simply saying to a group, "We're looking for ways to speed up production. What suggestions do you have?" People with insecurities may lay low, people with agendas may snipe at others, and people with creative ideas may be ridiculed. Your opening lines can set the scene for success by encouraging respect, risk-taking, and fun. Something like, "We're here to kick around ways to speed up production. Let's use some ground rules for good brainstorming: More ideas are better, every voice in here is important, questions should be for

clarification not criticism, and the only ideas we should laugh at are mine!"

4. **The call to the home.** When it's necessary to contact employees at home, your opening line shouldn't be about business. It should be an acknowledgment that you're on their time and an appreciation of their help. Learn the names of your employees' spouses or significant others so you can address them personally. (There's no shame in keeping a list to help your memory.) When I first became a news director in the 1970s, the majority of my employees were men who had always worked for men. I made a special point to learn about their families. When I called to roust someone from bed in the middle of the night to chase breaking news, I wouldn't just say, "May I speak to John?" It would be, "Hi Connie, it's Jill from the station. I'm sorry to wake you but there's a major fire and we need to send John. May I speak with him?" It wasn't some ice-cold "other woman" on the line, demanding access to their spouse, but a friendly professional acknowledging a disruption of their lives. (I did the same for the women on staff and their husbands, too.)

Remember, of course, that whatever your opening line, your tone and delivery are equally important. That point was driven home by an employee on the tech side of a business, a self-described "old guy" who'd seen more than his share of bosses in his long career. His latest supervisor was many years his junior and overseeing lots of changes in the operation. That's often a recipe for tension and resistance. Instead, the veteran and other crew members gave her high marks for her skill, her organization, and most of all her clear and upbeat communication. He wrote in her feedback:

You'd be surprised how disarming a sincere smile can be. A fake smile can be seen from 27½ feet away. Honest. But when someone is positive inside and it flows out through their eyes and mouth you can see it a mile away...I'm informed in a timely way of all changes. I know what she expects from me. I know what my duties are. I know people respect her. I know she is doing the job right. That's damn close to perfect. Amen.

"Amen" is right; it's damn close. But you can get closer. Let's look at the *end* of the communications you're learning to *start* so well.

Hey! Close the Loop!

I wrote that header so that it sounded like a shout. This lesson is that important: If you want to be known as a great boss, be absolutely vigilant about closing the loop in your communications. Be the manager who rarely keeps people hanging for answers or unclear about next steps. While it sounds simple, the complaints I hear suggest that this is an art too many managers have yet to master.

Bosses who fail to follow through, or do it in slow motion, cause frustration, anxiety, and wasted time for their staff. And I'm not talking about egregious sins like breaking promises or consistently blowing important deadlines. I'm talking about smaller, everyday lapses—missed opportunities to close the loop. Have you experienced situations like this?

You send an email to a colleague: "Could we get together for a few minutes tomorrow to review the budget change?"

Your coworker's reply: "Sorry, I'll be at an off-site meeting all day."

You received half an answer to your question: "No" for tomorrow. "Yes" for...who the heck knows? The information loop is left hanging open. You're frustrated. Now you have to go back, nagging or begging. If not tomorrow, when?

Let's look at the same scenario with a *slightly* better response:

You: "Could we get together for a few minutes tomorrow to review the budget change?"
Colleague: "Sorry, I'll be at an off-site meeting all day. I'll get back to you."

The promise to reply sometime is better than the first message, but not by much. The loop's still open. You're still on hold, with no way of knowing how long. You're left with the choice of pushing back for specificity or waiting—probably doing a slow burn as you do.

When people commit to closing the loop at every opportunity, responses look like this:

"Sorry, I'll be at an off-site meeting all day. I have to double-check, but I think I'm open between nine and eleven the following morning. If that works for you, I'll get you an answer before end of business today."

The message is clear. Your request matters; the response proves it. To make it matter even more, I'd suggest delivering it on the phone or face-to-face, rather than email, if that's possible.

I intentionally set up that scenario to feature you and a peer in your organization, not you and your supervisor. Now let's go there. It's bad enough when colleagues fail to close the loop, but it's especially problematic when the boss is the offender. Employees aren't especially comfortable telling bosses that they have chronic "bad communication breath" about closing loops. Rather than criticize the boss, they grumble and try to work around the information gaps, often adding needless extra work. They lose respect for their managers— all because the person with the power to answer a question, to respond to a request, to help them get something done, has left them hanging. They feel dissed, like the employee who wrote this feedback:

> *When someone calls or emails, try to get back to them in a reasonable time frame. Not answering a question from staff members or taking two or three days to get back is a problem.*

So don't cause needless problems. Close your loops. But don't make it your personal habit alone. Teach it to others. Tie it to important values you talk about: respect, collaboration, and effectiveness. In time, closure can become part of your team's culture, something that happens automatically.

Here's what it looks like in action on the job, according to the authors of the book *Built on Trust: Gaining Competitive Advantage in Any Organization*:

> Closure means coming to a specific agreement about what will be done, by whom, with a specific date for completion. You don't leave anyone dangling. "I'll get you the report" isn't closure because there's no time given... "I'll

do what I can" isn't closure because there's no specific agreement for what will be done.

In a culture of closure, if someone neglects the "what" or the "when," it's okay to tactfully respond, even to the boss, with a request for more specificity. In fact, employees can suggest alternative meeting times in the very first email to the boss ("Tomorrow—or if tomorrow's not good, then, how about..."), because aiming for closure is an automatic goal for everyone. Nobody's seen as needy or pushy; they're respectful and efficient.

So where else can closing the loop make a big difference? Think of a meeting you've attended that seemed like all talk and no action. Chances are it suffered from lack of closure. The leader didn't wrap it up—or didn't quickly follow it up—with a recap and a next-steps plan. At best it seemed like a waste of your time, at worst (especially if the issue on the table was important to you) it was deeply disappointing. In a culture of closure, people leave meetings understanding what was decided, what the next steps will be, who's doing what, by what deadlines.

How's your track record for closure? You might want to ask a few folks on your team for some feedback on your follow-through. If you're really good at it, I bet they'll get right back to you.

DANGER: EMAIL TRAPS AHEAD!

How will you know your team is achieving a culture of closure? One sign is that you'll be exchanging fewer emails. You'll need fewer back-and-forth messages to reach clarity. That's a good thing, because today's bosses are besieged by electronic messages. They're managing both the sheer volume and all the communication traps email presents. For that reason, I suggest that every boss develop an email strategy. It starts with a mission statement that guides your actions. Here's mine:

> I believe email is an effective tool for exchanging information but inferior to face-to-face interaction. I will use it for positive purposes like transferring knowledge, updating, connecting, and celebrating. I won't spam people, send incomplete messages that require more correspondence to clear them up, and will not use email as a letter bomb.

That philosophy emerged from seeing how many managers mishandle email, and the traps that lead to email misunderstandings. Here's my list:

Five Major Email Traps

1. Email can be tone-deaf.

It may deliver information without context. The reader can't see the writer's face, read body language, hear inflection or volume. Let's play a game with this question: "Is the computer fixed yet?" Using your best dramatic skills, read that question aloud three different ways. I'm betting one of your reads sounded friendly, one might have sounded like a cry for help, and one like an accusation. (Is the computer fixed *yet*?") You can avoid the trap of tone-deaf email by calling upon your newfound "opening lines" skills. The first line you write in an email sets the tone for how the recipient takes in the rest of the message. Instead of just asking the question, precede it with a tone-setting opening line. Those few seconds of extra keystrokes are a worthwhile investment of your time:

> Hi Omar. Hope all's well. Just touching base on one of your many projects: Is the computer fixed yet?

2. Email can become a substitute for human interaction.

Busy bosses can drift away from the very thing staffers want: opportunities to go face-to-face with the person in charge, to ask questions, get feedback, and feel they've been heard. Smart bosses don't equate sending a message with making a high-quality personal connection. Email can be a fine broadcast platform for singing the praises of a team's job well done. Everyone gets to read the message. But don't stop there, boss. Couple it with your in-person, real-time, look-'em-in-the-eye, give-'em-a-high-five communication. One manager, who was given credit for being very effective at sending information by email and text, was also nudged by a staffer with this advice:

> *Come out more and talk with us. People need a leader and leadership needs a person who can personally interact and communicate physically.*

3. Email can cause more work and confusion.

We all know the challenges of piling, filing, searching, and sorting email. Email writers add to the problem when they neglect to fill in subject lines, making later searches a struggle. (Why is it that I see this more often among managers than line workers? Rank does *not* have privilege on this one. Do the work!) How about when bosses "cc" and forward messages without explanation, leaving recipients to wonder, "Why was I copied on this message? Am I part of some problem? Some solution? Am I supposed to act on this or just read it?"

4. Email from bosses can seem urgent, even when it's not.

Bosses are often surprised to learn the unintended impact of their messages. Remember those rules you never knew you made? You probably never told people, "I expect you to stop whatever you're doing when you get an email from me." But that's what they may assume. In the absence of clear direction or context, they'll disrupt their day and juggle their priorities in an effort to comply with your "rule." Just a few extra words like "by Monday," "no rush," or "I'm on deadline, could I get this right away?" can really help them budget time and effort.

5. Email is forever.

I advise managers to craft memos and emails with the assumption that they could be published online—or on the front page of the morning paper—for all the world to see. Could you, the author, look like a bully, boor, or bozo? Answer: Yes. It's the price you pay for using email like a heat-seeking missile. Settle your conflicts face-to-face.

Try a technique that one self-aware, self-managing boss

passed along to me. To break her habit of sending "nasty grams" when stressed, she says to herself, in the tone of a highway patrolman, "Ma'am, step away from the keyboard."

NOW, LET'S LOOK INTO YOUR EARS

Great bosses know that healthy communication isn't simply about what comes *out of* their brains, their typing fingers, and their mouths. It's also about what goes *into* their ears. I'm talking about listening skills. This is another one of those management competencies that can only be judged by others, not by you. No matter what *you* think of your listening abilities, it's your staff that decides whether they feel heard and understood when talking to you.

It's often said that successful employees "have the boss's ear." But ears aren't enough. They want your eyes, too, dear manager. And when they're with you, they want your full focus. Simply put, if you want to be known as a good listener, here's a shortcut to success: Take your pinkies off the computer keys. Put down the BlackBerry. Turn your whole self in the direction of the person speaking to you. Look 'em in the eye (but not continuously, that's creepy). I guarantee if you try those small steps, you will improve your reputation as a listener.

I know because of the number of complaints I hear about multitasking bosses who tell staffers, "Go ahead, talk, I'm listening." But the employees hear, "Here's a fraction of my attention, that's plenty." Employees don't like it. And I don't blame them. I also don't blame good bosses who are trying to do many things at once. They're probably overloaded themselves and feel it's better to be accessible while otherwise engaged than to say, "I don't have time for you."

I *do* blame managers who expect people to adapt to their quirks—like short attention spans, faulty time management, or inscrutable priorities. Rank may have its privileges, but being rude and expecting people to endure that isn't one of them. Call me an eternal optimist, but I think the rude crowd is small. Most lousy listeners don't intend to offend. And when they learn they're seen that way, they're humbled, hurt, and open to change.

What else can they do besides disconnect from their electronic tethers? They can follow the lead of the managers whose feedback tells them they're excellent listeners. Here are some quick tips:

• **Pause whatever you're doing.** Make it obvious that you are fully focused. You might step out from behind your desk, or let a ringing phone go to voice mail.

• **Check your body language.** Are you inclined in the direction of the speaker or away? If someone snapped a photo of the two of you, what message would the picture suggest? Tension? Distance? Collaboration? Camaraderie?

• **Resist the temptation to interrupt the other person.** It's especially important if he or she has just begun to speak. The exception, of course, is when you're truly helping people by informing them that a problem has already been solved or a major worry they're expressing is groundless. But still, hear them out after your interruption. There's always more to a story.

- **Repeat what you heard.** This is another solid-gold way of getting credit for listening. If you can reiterate their message, they know you've paid attention.

- **Reflect on their feelings.** "Sounds like you're pretty pumped about the assignment" and "It's pretty clear you're concerned about the timetable" let people know you didn't just hear their words, you understood the emotions behind them.

- **Be up-front about how much time you have for a conversation.** If you have only ten minutes, it's best to tell the other person. If you are expecting a call you absolutely must take, give a warning about the unfortunate but unavoidable interruption to come. One practical tip—keep a timepiece somewhere in easy line of sight in your workspace, letting you keep track of time without doing the obvious watch check that appears to say, "Are you done yet? I *so* want this to be over."

Being a better listener doesn't mean you have to give up control of your time or become a slave to windbags. It means developing a workable strategy for making yourself available and then giving people your full focus when you're with them. The benefit: Your staff members feel you treat them with respect. You'll rank right up there with this rock star listener:

He always finds time to talk, even if it takes a while, because of meetings and all the manager stuff he has to deal with. He will make a point to meet. And he takes time to let the conversation go where it needs to. He doesn't sit and look at the clock. He always feels completely engaged. He listens very well, and one of the things that he does I really like is he reacts to what you're telling him. He tells you how it makes him feel, the things it reminds him of.

Didn't I tell you that nothing you say or do goes unnoticed?

Check Yourself: Is There a "Communication Doctor" in the House?

Here's an exercise I've used when teaching leadership in organizations. I ask the managers to break into small groups. Their assignment: Identify the top three communicators among all the managers in their organization, *and tell me what those managers* do *to earn that distinction.* Please note that the emphasis is on specific **behavior**, not "qualities." It's not enough to say people are considerate or creative or clear. We need to identify the things these people do **differently and better** than others. There's always a lot of buzz in the small groups. When they report out their findings, they usually identify the same people.

We make a list of those managers and the noteworthy things they do. They become our "communication doctors." Since they are right there in the room (surprised to have been singled out for praise), I invite them to share the why and the how of their communication successes.

With such rich natural resources already on the team, why don't people do this kind of sharing on their own? Because it often takes an outsider's encouragement to make it safe and fun to talk about. So let me encourage you to try this exercise with your team. Identify the communication doctors in your house. Then listen and learn.

Oh, and if you're tempted to say you don't have time for that—read on. The next chapter will help you find that time!

CHAPTER 6

To Win the Battle for Your Time, Talk Back to the Voices in Your Head

Quick quiz question: What manager said, "I am a rock star when it comes to managing time"?

Answer: No one.

Really.

I've worked with thousands of bosses, and even the most organized say they fight a constant battle to control their time. They're just like you: too many duties and not enough minutes in the day. They're on a quest for tips to become more effective. Here's the best tip I can offer you:

Time management doesn't start with your calendar. It starts with the voices in your head—and learning how to talk back to them. For better or worse, those voices guide the choices you make about how you spend your time and energy.

There's one very unhelpful voice I want you to tackle first. It's the one that whispers to bosses:

"Today's the day they find out you really don't deserve this job."

Sound familiar? It's known as "impostor syndrome"—the nagging notion that you're more lucky than talented. Even great bosses suffer from this kind of self-second-guessing. The dangers of the impostor phenomenon were first written about by clinical psychologists Pauline Clance and Suzanne Imes back in 1978. They studied its effects on professional women. Further research revealed that the syndrome is equally common among men. I've seen proof. In workshops, I'll talk about the voice that taunts bosses—"today's the day they find you out"—and ask who's heard it. All across the room, seemingly confident guys and gals raise their hands. You should see the relief on their faces. Until that moment, most assumed they were the lone impostor in the house.

What's the connection between this voice and time management? It's huge. Impostor syndrome can make you compulsive about working harder and putting in longer hours than anyone else, to prove that you really deserve your role. It can cause you to neglect the tasks you're less good at, because you fear that even a small failure might unmask your overall "unworthiness." You may cling to the duties you do well, whether or not they are the most important among your responsibilities, because they provide you a cover of competence. Until you silence that impostor voice, it can leave you exhausted, inefficient, and ineffective.

There are other voices in your head. They may be the words of your parents, teachers, past bosses, or even some Evil Twin of yours. They say things like, "The person in charge should be the first to arrive and the last to leave," or "Never keep your boss waiting," or "You can't fight the system."

The voices in your head inevitably influence the three main fronts on the battle to control your time:

- **Demands:** Your responsibilities as you know them and the priorities you set.
- **Assumptions:** What you believe your bosses expect from you and what you think good managers are supposed to do.
- **Preferences:** The way you like to work; your comfort zones.

Duties, **assumptions**, and **preferences**—let's shorthand them with the acronym **DAP**. Each person's DAP profile is unique. That's because organizations, bosses, and employees vary. Our voices, values, and habits vary. That's why the best teaching of time management is custom-tailored. Ideally, your time management coach would ask you lots of questions. Your answers would then lead you to some discoveries and ultimately to making some important choices and changes in how you operate.

Let's do that right now. Grab a pen (or a sheet of paper, in case you don't want to mark up your book). It's time to conduct your **DAP audit**.

YOUR DAP AUDIT

Please answer my series of pushy personal questions about your duties, assumptions, and preferences. If they make you uncomfortable, it means we're doing something right. My goal is to get you to think critically about the many choices you make each day (and the voices that may drive them). Following each question, you'll see an "**action**" line. It means, "Based on what you've answered, what are you going to do?" Those "action" notes are the payoff to this exercise, because they will lead you to make an overall plan. Let's start:

YOUR DEMANDS

1. **What is the most important contribution you make to your organization as a boss—the most important work you do? What kind of conversations do you have with your boss about this?**

Action:

_____

_____

_____

2. **What percentage of the tasks you do each day deal directly with that "most important work you do" in your organization? If the percentage isn't what**

you'd like, what's getting in your way? What might you do about it?

Action:

_____

_____

_____

3. **What duties do you have that you and you alone handle? How important are they and how much of your time do they take? What duties do you handle simply because no one else knows how to do them? What could you do about that?**

Action:

_____

_____

_____

4. **Which of your staffers seem to take up a disproportionate amount of your time? Low performers? High performers? New employees? If you see a pattern, what does it tell you and what might you do about it?**

Action:

_____

(Continued)

_____

_____

5. **What deadlines are an immovable part of your work and what impact do they have on the way you schedule your time? How well do you schedule all your other responsibilities around those deadlines? Could you do better?**

Action:

_____

_____

_____

6. **What "weak links" in your organization cause a drain on your time (flawed or nonexistent systems, unclear roles, poor communication, etc.), and how might they be strengthened? How could you help?**

Action:

_____

_____

_____

Reviewing Your Demands

The goal here is for you to get crystal clear about the biggest contributions you bring to your job—and what your boss specifically expects of you. Only then can you develop your personal time management strategy. Instead of simply reacting to whatever pops up in front of you each day, you prioritize. You decide what to *stop* doing, do less of, or do more of. You choose what you will delegate to others. You focus more attention on people who bring the most value to your team. You reexamine systems and workflow to look for time bandits.

YOUR ASSUMPTIONS

1. **What's your first reaction to the word "delegation"? Is it a concept you are comfortable or uncomfortable with? Why? Can you identify work you might delegate to others, and people on your team who are good candidates for the opportunity?**

Action:

_____

_____

_____

2. **What do you believe your boss expects of you when it comes to things like: your availability to him/her, your attendance at meetings of all types, your ability to make independent decisions, the amount**

(Continued)

of delegation you do, the kind of hours you work, etc.? Is there more information, clarification, or change you'd like from your boss? What might you do about that?

Action:

_____

_____

_____

3. Are there traditional and time-consuming protocols or paperwork in your workplace that you and others complain about or struggle with? What are they—and when was the last time you and colleagues brainstormed alternatives?

Action:

_____

_____

_____

4. What are your assumptions about underperforming employees and your role in handling them? How much of your time is taken up dealing with problem people and performance? What might you like to change?

Action:

_____

_____

_____

5. **What are your assumptions about the kind of work ethic a manager should model for the team? How do your assumptions affect the start and end times of your days, the length of your weeks, or the quality of your time off? What might you do about that?**

Action:

_____

_____

_____

Reviewing Your Assumptions

The goal here is to make you an investigative reporter—digging for facts instead of listening to the voices in your head or your best guesses. When you get the facts, you might be less apt to see delegating as risky business. You won't assume your bosses are giving orders when they might be simply making observations. You'll challenge old ways of doing things. And you'll make certain you aren't spending

(Continued)

more time with poor performers than with your top talent. You might even determine that you don't need to be tethered to technology 24/7. You'll schedule your time based on facts, not fears.

YOUR PREFERENCES

1. **Do you prefer tasks that involve personal interactions? Or do you work better when you can step away from people, so you can think? How does that preference affect the way you schedule your time—for better or worse? What might you modify?**

Action:

_____

_____

_____

2. **Are there parts of your job that you like so much that you usually do them first or often, even if they aren't a priority for the organization? What's the impact of that—positive or negative? What might you change without taking away all your joy?**

Action:

_____

_____

_____

3. Is there work you did before becoming a manager that you continue to do because it's satisfying to you and demonstrates your competence? If so, how does this affect your other responsibilities? What could you do about that?

Action:

_____

_____

_____

4. Are you a "planner" who loves making lists and beating deadlines by a mile? Are you a "plunger" who loves to keep options open, thinks lists are unnecessary, and finds the time right before deadline the most energizing? How does your preference affect your time management and that of others on your team? What kind of conversations have you had with others about the impact of your work habits?

Action:

_____

(Continued)

_____

_____

5. **How do you use technology to help manage your time? Are you cutting-edge or old-school about tech tools? Is there more you'd like to learn? What's in your way and how could you remove those barriers?**

Action:

_____

_____

_____

Reviewing Your Preferences

Have you distinguished which preferences make you happy and successful at work and which are messing with your ability to get your work done efficiently and effectively? Are your "people person" tendencies keeping you from tackling important paperwork? If you love solitude, are you neglecting the all-important "management by walking around"? As much as you might hate lists, are you losing track of deadlines and duties? Get really honest with yourself about what you can let go of and what you need to learn, especially when it comes to labor-saving technology. Don't let your anxiety about learning keep you working with outdated tools. Expand your comfort zone.

Putting It All Together into an Action Plan

Listen carefully to *my* voice: Your "Action" notes are your blueprint for solving challenges by making choices. Now it's time to turn them into a real plan, one that includes long- and short-term goals, recruits some allies, sets timetables for completion and measurements of success.

I've learned that when people put things into plan form—and let people know they've done it—it helps them stay committed to it.

A special word to self-doubters or procrastinators: You can do this—right now. I'll help. I promise to fill the rest of this book with advice to help you reach the goals you've set. And I developed a simple planning grid to make it easier for you, something you can refer back to as we move forward.

DAP AUDIT ACTION PLAN	
What?	**Who?**
What do I want to improve? Short term—things I can do right away: Longer term—things that are bigger projects:	Who will be my allies in this adventure? Whose help is critical to the success? Who has a stake in the improvement?

DAP AUDIT ACTION PLAN *(Continued)*	
When?	**How?**
What's my timetable for the things I want to accomplish, short and long term? What reasonable deadlines should I set for myself so I stay on track?	How will I measure success in a real, tangible way? How will I celebrate my victories in the battle for my time?

Let's proceed with the help I promised as you move forward on your goals.

DELEGATION DO'S AND DON'TS

I've encouraged you to become better at delegation, because it's a gap for most managers. I want you to become as proficient as this boss, about whom a colleague wrote:

> *He never rests on his laurels and is always seeking ways to improve our performance, even as resources contract and the pressure on staff increases. He is not afraid to delegate; he stands back and lets you get on with it, but he is always close at hand, seeking updates on how the job is going, asking if assistance is needed.*

As you can see, that boss has figured out the right balance of sharing responsibilities, while keeping appropriately light oversight. To help you become more like him, here are my top tips.

Do: Review your staff and the duties you want to start delegating. Start being a matchmaker. Choose people who are ready for the next challenge and who like to solve problems. This is important: Tell them *why* you've selected them for the assignment. It's wonderful feedback on their competence.

Don't: Delegate and disappear. Keep connected so you can give feedback and help. Make certain to let people know that you intend to do this not because you want to micromanage, but because you want to be a resource and cheerleader for their success. On time-sensitive projects, delegate with deadlines.

Do: Delegate projects and duties that help staffers raise their profile in the organization. Great bosses use delegation to help employees build both their skills and their reputations. Share the spotlight. When they look good, you look good.

Don't: Feel guilty when handing over a task you're not crazy about. Don't assume you are dumping instead of delegating. We're all different. Another person might enjoy the work more than you—and improve on it. If the person doesn't like the task any more than you do—you can still delegate it. As a boss, you have the right to distribute all the work, even that which is the least desirable. Just be fair about it and be sure to show appreciation.

And one final "Do" that is essential to effective delegation: When you want good people to learn and grow, delegate—but provide them sufficient information and authority so they'll succeed.

There's a massive difference between delegating *work* to an employee and delegating *responsibility and authority* to that person. Delegation functions best when you give people power to make decisions regarding the assignment. Without it, they can feel like your remote-controlled robots. With it, they're thinkers and doers. People get much more invested in projects when they've had a role in shaping them. They are more likely to fall in love with ideas, solutions, and decisions of their own creation.

Having said that, I now must alert you to the times *you shouldn't delegate at all*. Sometimes because of time, effectiveness, or importance, you should simply tell people what you've decided and what they must do. It's called the top-down or command-and-control style of management.

When Should You Forgo Delegation and Stick with DIY?

Command-and-control managers don't delegate, they dictate. I'm not a fan of this style—and neither are employees—under most circumstances. But there are important exceptions, times when "I'm the boss, do exactly what I've decided" is the *perfect* approach. The trick is to know when and why you should decide it yourself.

When to DIY—Decide It Yourself—and *Not* Delegate

The situation is urgent and you have a high level of expertise.

There's a breaking business challenge or opportunity. Time is of the essence. You have an excellent grasp of the issues and know that in making the decision, you won't be stunned by unintended or unexpected consequences. In this situation, you don't waste time. You don't delegate. You decide.

People are in conflict and unwilling or unable to resolve matters themselves.

In healthy organizations, people usually work things out without dragging the boss into a dispute. But when they can't or don't, you must make the judgment call. Warning: If this happens often, you are wasting your time being a referee instead of a leader. Invest your time building a culture of constructive conflict resolution, setting expectations, and teaching people how to resolve differences without you. (More on that later!)

People are tired or frightened and need an executive decision to empower them.

When a team is demoralized by a setback, they need a confident, unequivocal call to action that says, "Do this now. I believe in you." Sometimes they need your permission to take care of themselves.

Allow me to share a personal story: When our first child was born prematurely at 2 pounds, 12 ounces, my husband and I kept watch at his bedside in the neonatal intensive care unit late into the night, every night. We just didn't want our tiny Noah to see us leave him, so we'd wait until he'd fall asleep before taking our long ride home. (Imagine the voices in our heads, telling us what good parents must do!) At one point during Noah's long stay, one of his NICU doctors sized up our apparent exhaustion and gave us an order:

"Go home and get more sleep. It's best for you and your son." It took an authority figure's direction to override the voices in our heads. Only then did we give ourselves permission to rest.

Your people may need the same kind of voice of authority to decide what's best for them when their own thinking may be clouded by exhaustion, by fear, or by uncertainty.

The decision carries a high degree of risk for the decision-maker.

Sometimes you need to make a call that involves major expense, bending the rules, or trying an unorthodox approach. It could work well or it might backfire big time. Great bosses don't delegate decisions that could harm the decision-maker. They assume the risk themselves. It's a way of demonstrating both care and courage to your staff.

How Do You Learn to "Just Say No"?

Another time management challenge for managers is their inability or reluctance to turn down requests for their time. Why do we say yes to assignments, tasks, or favors when no is really a better option? Here are some reasons:

- We're workhorses, proud of our ethic; we say, "Bring it on, we can handle it."
- We're pleasers; we feel guilty when we disappoint others.
- We're ambitious; we may become more valuable by doing the requested task.

- We're egotistical experts; we like being the best person for the job.
- We're networkers; we believe helping colleagues builds important bonds.
- We're plungers, not planners; we react to requests without full consideration of our calendars.

Which of those sound most like your reasons? Figuring out what drives your reluctance to reject a request is the first step toward formulating a strategy for weeding out unproductive activities. Look at your reasons and ask yourself:

- How has this helped me?
- How has this hurt me?
- What am I not getting done in my professional and personal life because I say yes for the wrong reasons?

Your strategy for saying no should start with a look at important reasons to, in fact, accept whatever responsibility has been offered you. If what you're being asked to do is directly connected to the main responsibilities of your job, if it helps you demonstrate important leadership and success, if it is something only you can and should do, then do it. It's also wise to embrace the request if it provides you an extraordinary learning opportunity, the chance to build valuable social capital with your boss or a key colleague, or offers meaningful service to your community.

If the request doesn't meet those criteria, you have options:

- **Delegate** (Pass it on.)
- **Collaborate** (Share the task with others.)

- **Negotiate** (Offer to do something else that fits with your time and priorities, or agree to stop doing something so you can comply with the request.)
- **Decline** (Say some variation of "No thanks.")

But when the answer is no, how do you find the right words to decline? You don't want to offend the requesting person, but you also don't want to sound so conflicted that you allow yourself to be talked back into yes.

One key thing to remember is that you don't always have to give a detailed reason when you decline. Some folks really struggle with this, feeling like they need some airtight alibi to prove their innocence to the authorities. Well, if you are indeed dealing with "authorities"—your bosses or key managers—then by all means provide reasons that verify both your goodwill and bad schedule. (We'll talk more in chapter 14 about your relationship with your boss, because I know this is a critical part of managing not only your time but your career.)

For requests from others, you may simply and politely say, "I'm really sorry, but I just can't fit that into my schedule," or "I have to take a pass on your request this time, but I want to help you in the future." Your firm but friendly tone will be a big help.

In her book *Time Management from the Inside Out*, author Julie Morgenstern advises rehearsing your no's:

> If you're not used to it, prepare some answers in advance and memorize them. That way you won't be caught off guard and find the words "Yes, of course I will" popping out of your mouth...Practice saying "I'm sorry, I just can't" and "No" out loud. Say them with firmness and conviction until they feel natural.

You'd be surprised at how often managers in my seminars get feedback from colleagues that encourages them to delegate more and learn to say no. It looks like this:

I do think she is sometimes "too available." In addition to the effect on her personally, some employees use it as a crutch to avoid making decisions (myself included!).

I'm not sure that saying no is ever going to feel natural for those of us who gravitate more naturally toward yes. But for the sake of our effectiveness as leaders, for the benefit of our work teams and our personal lives, it's time for us to get more positive about the occasional—and strategic—negative.

Memorize This Final, Vital Time Management Tip

As you move forward on the action plan from your DAP audit, I leave you with a tip that has proved helpful to many managers I've taught. It's simply this:

If you're serious about getting something accomplished, schedule it.

That's because scheduled time drives out unscheduled time. Scheduling protects you from other temptations and provides the excuse for saying no to other requests.

If you've decided to teach people how to do some of the work you're now doing, put that training on everyone's calendar. If you want to start meeting regularly with your mid-level managers to give them more responsibilities, lock in the meeting times. If you want to stop working crazy hours and start exercising more, sign up for a class that makes you leave work at a reasonable hour. Again, listen to my voice: Scheduling changes a "wish" into a "plan."

Take one last look at your DAP audit action plan. What might you take from that and turn into a commitment so important that you schedule it? Let that be the voice that guides you.

☽

Our next stop on your road to becoming a great boss takes us to the land of managing people—all sorts of people. When you become very good at that, you'll get feedback like this:

He's clear about his expectations and assessments, which is one reason he earns respect from people who do lots of different jobs. He has an uncanny eye for talent—as good as anyone. He appreciates a wide range of skill sets and cheerfully tolerates a huge range of eccentricities. And in the rare event an employee is not able to succeed, despite many interventions, he is willing to do the hard work of showing problem employees the door.

Read on. I promise to make all the hard work of managing people much easier for you.

Section Two

All About Your Staff
How Great Bosses Grow Great Employees

CHAPTER 7

You Should *Not* Treat Everyone the Same

Great bosses know that the most important thing they do is help employees succeed.

If I had an ounce of needlework talent I would turn that message into a sampler. If I were a graffiti artist, I'd tag buildings with it. If I sported a tattoo...naw, let's not go there.

That message about employee success is my immediate response when asked what sets the best bosses apart from the rest. I want to burn it into your brain because it represents a new mindset for high achievers like you.

Chances are, you were an impressive employee before moving into management. You racked up accolades for your accomplishments. Now it isn't about *you* anymore—it's about the people on your team. You've moved from being a star soloist to the conductor of the symphony orchestra.

You can get some beautiful music out of your employee ensemble if you avoid two dangerous fallacies:

- **Fallacy Number One:** You help employees succeed by teaching them to work just like you.
- **Fallacy Number Two:** You must treat everyone the same.

I know those ideas *seem* to make sense. You did a lot of things right when you were the "doer," and it got you promoted, so why not have people copy you? And how in the world can you be known as fair-minded if you don't manage everyone the same way?

The answer is simple: Every person is different, just like the instruments in an orchestra. What they have in common is that *they aren't you*. If you try to make them your clones, they'll flounder. And if you treat each person identically, you're inviting your Evil Twin to undermine you. Instead of being seen as the Manager Who's Mighty Fair, you'll be seen by many as the Manager Who's Making Me Fail.

How do you learn to treat employees differently but still be true to your goal of fair play? You get smart about the fascinating and frustrating array of differences among perfectly normal people.

Let's start with personalities, the core of who we are. I'll use descriptions from the Myers-Briggs Type Indicator, which I use in my teaching. In fact, I always follow our 360-feedback sessions by teaching about personality preferences and differences, because it helps managers understand why various employees can view a boss's behaviors in completely contrasting ways—and what they can do about it. We'll launch our look at personalities by focusing on introverts and extroverts.

Introverts and Extroverts: More Than Meets the Eye (and Ear)

Travel back in time with me to my first management job. I was a sixteen-year-old-clerk at (no kidding) Kissin' Cuzzins Country Candy Store in downtown Milwaukee. That summer, my boss was needed at a second location and suddenly I was in charge. I quickly learned about hiring, bookkeeping, inventory control, and customer service. I liked dealing with customers the best. I'm an extrovert, so chatting them up and handing out free candy samples was a treat for me.

Our store was adjacent to the Riverside Theater, so lots of our customers were moviegoers. Some of them arrived alone. I'd package up their chocolate, gumdrops, or licorice—and feel oh so sorry for them. Who but a desperately lonely person would go to a movie without a companion? As they made their solitary exits, I'd sigh.

Now I know I was wasting my breath—and my sympathy. When I tell that story to introverts today, the nicest ones laugh at me and others just shake their heads. Why couldn't I consider the possibility that the lone moviegoers were having a wonderful time?

Because I was seeing the world through an extrovert's lens.

Extroverts like me get their energy from the outer world of connecting with people. They "power up" in the company of others. At the end of a long day of talking with others at work, they want to go home—and talk about it. For extroverts, the quiet experience of viewing a movie is enhanced by the mere presence of another person. Of course, that extrovert will start chatting about the film even before the house lights come up.

Now you can see why I couldn't imagine people enjoying the theater experience alone. But introverts can, and they do. **Introverts** get their energy from the life of the mind. They are comfortable with solo activities and silence. While not as chatty as extroverts, they have plenty of ideas to share. They just prefer to process them fully before presenting them. They may have extensive, deep conversations with colleagues and other people close to them, but get less enjoyment out of making small talk in a room full of strangers. The ad-libbing drains their energy. At the end of a long day of talking on the job, they want to go home and recharge their batteries with a little quiet time. In the turnabout-is-fair-play department, introverts may feel sorry for people who just can't enjoy a movie without an escort in tow!

Each of us—introverts or extroverts—can misjudge the other. Think about the impact that can have on the way we manage people.

Take hiring, for example. Bosses are often tempted to hire in their own image. You know how that goes: "She reminds me of myself when I first started here," or "We really clicked." We're attracted to people who seem like a reflection of us.

Unless you expand your understanding and appreciation of differences, you may miss out on hiring some terrific people who fill in your gaps—and you'll make unwise decisions as you evaluate, train, and promote your employees.

So pick up your baton and learn to conduct your orchestra—starting with the quiet performers.

Insights into Working with Introverts

Introverts make up about half of the U.S. population, according to various estimates. But among management ranks, the balance shifts. Extroverts are more likely to be running things, and *not* because they are more intelligent. It's their willingness to step forward and speak out that propels them into the management pipeline, where schmoozing and cheerleading and off-the-cuff speaking are expected and rewarded. Make no mistake, there are plenty of successful introverted bosses. But with more extroverts in the driver's seat, it's especially important for all managers to understand and appreciate introverts.

Knowing that introverts get their energy from the life of the mind will make you less likely to confuse their understated approach with shyness, aloofness, or lack of ideas. You'll help them succeed by knowing what to expect from them and what they need from you.

Introverts are more likely than extroverts to be good listeners.

We've already talked about the importance of listening. This valuable skill can give introverts an advantage in many aspects of work and life, and bring benefits to your team. Introverts can make good workplace coaches, mentors, and mediators—all of which require intense listening. Many introverts have told me that before they were promoted to management, they often served as a sounding board for coworkers who wanted a safe place to explore ideas. Their willingness to listen builds trust—and their credibility. If you're an extrovert, you may not give introverts full credit for this gift because you value talking over listening.

Introverts may not be the first to speak in a group. So what?

If you ask a question or solicit suggestions, don't fall into the trap of assuming the first people to answer are the most enthusiastic and others must be "holding back." The introverts in your group are listening and formulating their ideas. They share them later in a meeting or conversation, and that can be a real benefit to the team. Often, they have been taking in all points of view and will helpfully synthesize what they heard, while adding their perspective. Be prepared for the likelihood that introverts will come to you with additional thoughts *after* a meeting, because they've continued to reflect on the topic. Instead of being irritated ("Why the heck didn't you say that in the conference room?"), bosses can seek out introverts after a meeting to mine those thoughts.

Introverts can get weary in meetings that wander.

It happens when the extroverts do what extroverts do: think out loud, repeat themselves, repeat what others say, and extend the event with all that chatter. If you're an extrovert running the meeting, you might think more talk is better talk, while your introverts are hoping you'll edit things down to the essentials. If you want to run efficient and effective meetings, I suggest you talk with your introverts about how to keep things moving without cutting off creativity or camaraderie. They often have good suggestions.

Introverts appreciate a heads-up.

They like to know about upcoming meeting agendas or conversation topics. It gives them time to reflect before speaking. They're not scared; they simply like to be prepared. The added bonus of agendas is that they are more likely to keep the chatty extroverts focused. You can also alert people at the beginning of a meeting that you want to make sure all voices are heard, and that you'll go around the table before you wrap up, so everyone can weigh in. That simple warning lets people know when to be ready.

Introverts may be less inclined to work a room.

In addition to avoiding small talk, introverts may also prefer email exchanges to face-to-face chats. It just seems more efficient and less draining to them. That means you, as the boss, need to determine when those habits impede communication or collaboration and give them guidance. You also need to let them know if their self-imposed low profiles are too low and they're not getting credit for good work. You can help them expand their comfort zone without changing the essence of who they are. All it takes is an explanation and some encouragement from you.

Introverts might not be the first to come knocking at your door.

Introverts might not be as aggressive as extroverts in hitting you up for special assignments or promotions, or as familiar to you as the staffers who routinely drop by your desk to shoot the breeze. You'll make a big mistake if you think it means introverts aren't ambitious, or decide that people forfeit an opportunity for a good assignment by not "asking for the order." Make certain you *invite* people very directly to discuss opportunities with you, and then judge them on the quality of their work. If that work involves being more outgoing and vocal, let them know the requirements—rather than assuming they're not interested or able.

Introverts can surprise you.

It's also important to understand that introverts are quite capable of leading meetings, giving great presentations, and speaking at length about subjects that are important to them. The best proof I can offer: TV news anchors. They're all extroverts, right? Nope. For years, I've conducted leadership workshops for these professional public speakers, and *one out of every four* turns out to be an introvert. Those introvert anchors can still shine in the spotlight, ad-lib hours of breaking news, or charm a live audience. They just want a little quiet time when they're finished.

Let's go back to your role as symphony conductor and hear from your louder players—the extroverts.

Insights into Working with Extroverts

We've already established that extroverts get energy from personal interactions. When you understand what makes them tick, you're less likely to see their outgoing approach as egotistical, pushy, or scatterbrained. You can help them channel their energy into positive outcomes. Some observations:

Extroverts are often the first to speak at a meeting and may say more than others.

Extroverts can make a room lively, but they can also dominate it, sometimes without even knowing it. When they think they've got the germ of a good idea, they want to get it out into the open to develop it. As they hear themselves talk, they keep fleshing out their thoughts. Now multiply that by several ideas and you can see how easily extroverts' words can expand to fill a meeting. It's up to you, the group leader, to encourage the participation of everyone. You can say things like, "I see a few hands up. Let's go to folks we haven't heard from yet," or "I'm going to ask you (extrovert) to hold that thought, because I fear we'll run out of time before we get to everyone." If you have some especially verbose employees, don't just play defense during meetings. You owe them some honest, constructive feedback about how they'll enhance their contribution to meetings by doing more self-editing.

Extroverts are often comfortable speaking before a group.

When extroverts are on project teams and it's time to make presentations, they'll be the ones leading the show. Their colleagues often delegate that role to them, knowing they'll represent the group well. I think it's good to play to people's strengths...to a point. As a boss, you need to make sure that this delegation doesn't become so automatic that it locks out others who might want the opportunity, or who would give it a try if you nudged them. Remember that management pipeline I talked about and how extroverts get a running start? Make sure your introverts get opportunities for the spotlight, too.

Extroverts talk well enough, but don't always listen well.

Extroverts often have to train themselves to listen patiently. For them, the words of writer Fran Lebowitz ring true: "The opposite of talking isn't *listening*. The opposite of talking is *waiting*." While that might sound selfish, it's not that simple. Extroverts just naturally want to jump in to connect with what they're hearing. They're apt to finish a speaker's sentence for them to prove, "I hear you! I know what you mean!" It's a gesture that's not universally appreciated, especially when the extrovert fills in the blanks too often or incorrectly. It's up to you to distinguish between irritating interruptions and enthusiastic exclamations—and coach your extroverts if they're getting in their own way.

Extroverts are good at working a room.

Extroverts can last only so long in an isolated work area. They need a "people fix" to stay energized, so expect to see them scouting for conversations. Again, you need to determine if that's wasting time or making them more effective. Extroverts are more likely than introverts to view group meetings as an effective way to get things done. You might not think your team needs to gather together to solve a problem or brainstorm, but if they're extroverts, that might be your best tactic. If you have an extrovert working at a remote location or telecommuting, know that they value keeping in touch, so stay connected.

Extroverts believe that talking things out is important.

If extroverted employees come to you with ideas or problems, they're praying you'll hear them out. Remember that they think by talking, so thinking through an issue doesn't mean going away somewhere to consider it; it means airing it. This doesn't mean you give up control of your time. You learn to guide those conversations. Tell employees how much time you have for the talk. Listen. Then tell the speakers what you've heard them say (or I guarantee they'll repeat it multiple times for you). Extroverts often think conversations should continue until they produce a decision. As a boss, you can let staffers know how you make decisions, and what the parameters of each talk will be, so there's no misunderstanding of how it will conclude.

Extroverts can surprise you.

Introverts may be better listeners by nature, but extroverts can develop the skill if they choose to. Lately, I've been pleased to see some very promising feedback given to extroverts. Here's an example of what was said about a manager who is quite high on the extrovert scale:

She's a fantastic listener, and talker, which we love.

This boss's skill set of listening and talking plays out in the way she leads a meeting, according to another staff member's feedback about her:

Although I don't have a lot to do with this part of the process, I recently was invited to sit in on one of our team's brainstorming meetings. It was an inspirational session because everyone really seemed to listen to one another's ideas and build upon them. As the leader, she seemed to gently guide the discussion toward ideas that seemed the most interesting, but no one was left out.

That manager knows how to conduct the symphony of personalities on her team, including her own.

I've explored the introvert/extrovert facets of personality in some depth to hammer home the importance of treating people differently in order to help them succeed, and why you can't assume they should or even could function just the way you do and still do their best work.

🌙

There are other facets of personality preference worth knowing about as you hone your strategies for managing people. Again, I'm drawing from my Myers-Briggs training and teaching. I'll give you a quick roundup, and I trust you'll spot yourself in some of these descriptions.

Detail or Big-Picture Person: Taking in Info

When I teach this session on how people take in information—through big pictures or small details—I use props. Sometimes I hold up a box of microwave popcorn. I ask the group to write down whatever comes into their heads as they see it. Some write, "She's holding a box of Orville Redenbacher's," or "Microwave popcorn. Box holds three packages." Those are the "sensing" folks. They take in information by focusing on the details, largely using their five senses. They tend to notice small things, like a dent in the box, or whether the popcorn is plain or butter-flavored.

Then there are the folks on the other end of the spectrum, who write things like, "It's Saturday night and we've rented a movie," or "Fatty snack foods contribute to the obesity problem in America." Those are the bigger-picture people, also known as "intuitors." They don't just see an object, they see concepts and contexts. They bypass the details and focus on meanings and abstractions. One of my favorite examples of this happened when I asked a group to write as I held up a box of Whitman's Sampler chocolates. (Hey, you can take the girl out of the candy store, but...) The sensors in the group wrote things like, "Yellow, one-pound box with old-fashioned lettering." But on the other side, a strong intuitor wrote, "She holds in her hands a box of forgiveness."

So what does this mean in terms of managing people?

- **Communication.** I hope you now understand why some people (intuitors) instinctively speak in metaphors and aren't being vague just to confuse you. You can appreciate why other people (sensors) are more "just the facts, ma'am" in what they say and what they'd like to hear. And you can tailor your messages accordingly.

- **Brainstorming.** I suspect you already know how easily brainstorming can go astray. For instance: You call a group of people together and ask them to toss out ideas for a new product. An intuitor starts ruminating about customer experiences and concepts rather than concrete things. A sensor on the team gets frustrated, hearing those generalities as blue-sky gibberish, and tries to shift the conversation to specific items. Pretty soon tensions rise and brainstorming shuts down. This explains why, as a leader, you must conduct that brainstorming orchestra with a little more finesse. You can tune them up by asking people to withhold the "How the heck could we make that work?" practical questions until after the group explores lots of possibilities. Or for a different type of gathering, you can state in advance that the goal is to come up with a fast, practical solution within specific budget limits. Those parameters nudge intuitors into sensing mode.

- **Managing change and new ideas.** Intuitors like revolution; they're comfortable blowing up old ways of doing things. Sensors like evolution; they prefer to adapt from the known. They're also "show me" people who want proof. In times of change or when facing new ways of thinking, sensors benefit from examples, analogies, and templates. True story: In my seminars, the intuitors tend to enjoy the Myers-Briggs sessions because they're drawn to the theories involved. The sensors often confess to me after class that they had been quite skeptical at the session's start—and the only way I won them over was to use role-playing exercises in which people's preferences played out as I predicted. For sensors, seeing is believing.

Hard-Liners and Soft Touches: Making Decisions

Another dimension of our personalities deals with how we make decisions. Some of us are known as tough but fair. We make our decisions by calculating the best route to a specific goal, using measurable facts and standards. We're pragmatic and businesslike. We're the "thinkers." Then there are others among us who make our decisions, first and foremost, through our personal values. We're idealistic and relationship-focused. We think first about the people who'll be affected by our decisions. We're known as kindhearted and stalwart about values. We're the "feelers."

If you're on the fence and not sure which you are, imagine you are responsible for work schedules (as you probably are). A good employee comes to you with a last-minute plea for an unscheduled day off. It's not a life-or-death situation, just a nice opportunity that's arisen—and would leave you short-staffed. If you're a thinker, you take an impersonal approach. You remind the employee of the rules and your need to be fair and consistent. You leave it to the employee to solve the problem by swapping shifts with a willing coworker, if there is one. If not, there's not much you can do.

If you're a feeler, you're more likely to get involved in the solution. You check to see if there's a way to say yes outright, since it's a good employee you don't want to disappoint. Failing that, you might help identify people who'd trade shifts. In extreme cases, you'll even work the shift yourself! (Let me add here that at some point, even feelers learn to shift into "thinker" mode when it comes to scheduling issues, because they'll burn themselves out with worry or work if they don't.)

Chances are, you have both thinkers and feelers on the team you lead. Your thinkers tend to be more competitive and by-the-book. Your feelers tend to be more cooperative but sometimes concerned about rules or plans that don't seem fair to all.

How does this affect the way you manage people?

• **Praise.** Thinkers are more likely to assume that praise is given for going over and above the call of duty: Why praise people for doing what they're supposed to do? They may seem stingy with compliments to their colleagues. Feelers view praise as care and concern: Why not praise people so they're encouraged to keep trying? They may seem like cheerleaders. When they work together, they may need you to translate them to each other. And when you praise them, you custom-tailor it. Thinkers want to know how they've scored, so tell them how they surpassed the standard. Use stats if it helps. Feelers also appreciate knowing how they've achieved, but respect means more to them if they also know they're liked.

- **Criticism.** For thinkers, it's truth before tact. They're not mean people, but for them, "what needs work" seems like a better place to start a critique than "what worked." For feelers, it's tact before truth, so they emphasize the positive first, and may sugarcoat their criticism. When thinkers and feelers work together, there's great potential for friction—and that's where you come in. Now that you know these are preferences, not character flaws, you can coach people to moderate the most extreme of their behaviors while retaining the best of them.

- **Social interactions.** Put the thinkers in charge of your staff softball team and they'll play to win, even if it means cutting some weak players. Put the feelers in charge and victory means everyone gets a turn at bat. When there's a birthday to be celebrated or a loss to be mourned, your feelers will take the lead in organizing a response, and they will expect support from you. The feelers on your staff are often your early warning system about morale issues. The thinkers on your staff are often the ones who nudge you to finally take action about an underperformer whom you've been too nice to confront.

Planners and Plungers: Some Love Scheduling, Others Love Serendipity

The last of the personality dimensions deals with the way we like to organize our lives. If we're "planners," we prefer order, organization, and predictability. We minimize uncertainty by looking ahead and charting a clear course. On the other hand, if we are "plungers," we prefer flexibility, serendipity, and keeping options open. We're more seize-the-moment people.

(For the record, the official Myers-Briggs terms are "judgers" and "perceivers," but "planners" and "plungers" seem to be more conversational handles, so I'll use those.)

Planners love making lists—sometimes even adding things just for the joy of checking them off! For them, lists provide peace of mind and help them monitor progress. Plungers may use lists but aren't fond of them. For them, lists simply offer protection against forgetting things, but they seem rigid and confining. Planners are more likely to keep organized files (and often neater workspaces), plungers more likely to have various piles (and often messier workspaces—but they usually can find whatever they need).

Once again, the question is, how does knowing this help you manage your staff more effectively?

• **Dancing with deadlines.** Give them an assignment, and both types will make deadline. But they will go about it in very different ways. Your planners will start thinking about it and taking some first steps sooner than your plungers will. They may nudge others to get started early with them, or at least talk about next steps. Their goal will likely be to finish the assignment before the deadline, with time to spare. They want the benefit of that extra time on the back end, just in case. To a planner, beating a deadline is the hallmark of a good worker. Your plungers are another story. They won't want to be pushed toward starting too early on a project. They want to group the work into a more compact and intense experience that starts much closer to the deadline. They get energized by deadlines and feel more focused by them. For plungers, turning in assignments well before deadline raises the risk of missed ideas and opportunities.

- **Work and play.** Planners and plungers may appear to have a different work ethic, when in reality they just take different routes to get things done. Here's the best example: In my workshops, I will ask the class to picture a line stretching from one end of a wall to the other. On one end of that line there's an imaginary sign that says, "Play begins when the work is finished." On the other end is a sign that says, "Play anytime; it helps the work." I ask people to go to the wall and position themselves wherever they feel most comfortable along that continuum. Inevitably, the planners cluster closer to the sign that puts work before play. Plungers gravitate toward the playful side. It's an eye-opening demonstration of diversity among successful professionals—and helps them understand each other much better. Remember, if you're their boss, you'd be standing somewhere on that line, too. Would you force everyone to adopt your preference? Or would you focus on the quality of the work and the workplace environment?

- **Team tension.** Since employees often work in teams, there can be a tug-of-war about whose preference should prevail, especially if people take their preferences to extremes. Planners can become too controlling. They may be so invested in the schedules that they resist good suggestions that come late in the game. Plungers may cause anxiety and real delays for other people involved in the workflow. Their playfulness at work may enhance creativity some days but be an annoying distraction on others. This is where they need you, the leader, to help them understand when their preferences get in their way. By setting clear standards (making sure you're not biased by your own preferences), you can help people move toward common ground, get things done, and work in harmony.

The Good News About Preferences and Performance

I have a confession to share with you now. When I first heard about personality preferences and profiles, I worried that they might be too simplistic—and, worst of all, might lock people into stereotypes. But having spent a good deal of time learning and teaching about them, I've come to appreciate how beneficial this knowledge can be. It's a powerful tool in that management toolkit of yours—as long as you remember my mantra: **Your preferences explain you, but they don't excuse you.** They reveal how we behave reflexively, but they don't lock in what we're capable of. They aren't a life sentence that forces us to behave only one way.

Here's a two-step exercise that symbolizes what I mean:

1. Would you kindly fold your arms?
2. Now, would you refold them so the other arm is on top?

How does that second effort feel? A little odd? You did the first fold automatically, almost without thinking. The second time, you took a second to think, and then you did it. It may not feel as comfortable, but you did just fine and could do it even more easily with practice. It's the same with personality preferences. Each of us can adapt when necessary. It just takes awareness, will, and effort.

Great bosses also know that we're the sum of much more than our personality types. We're diverse in gender, race, ethnicity, faith, sexual orientation, upbringing, geographic backgrounds, birth order, generational influences, life experiences—a long list of things that make each of us unique. Our chances of success increase when we work for bosses who know how to get the best out of who we are, who we can become, and **by not treating everyone the same.**

So, symphony conductor, lead on and read on. Our next stop is employee motivation—the core of happiness at work. I have some surprises for you.

CHAPTER 8

Work Happy: Motivation That *Really* Matters, Boss

Here's my fondest hope: As you are reading this book, the economy is robust, your organization is thriving, and your employees are well paid.

Would that be wonderful? You bet. But it's no guarantee your staff would be motivated or happy at work.

Surprised? Let me explain. Pay and benefits play an important role in motivation, but there's much more to the story—and that's why this chapter is so important. If you want to be a great boss, you need to master the kind of motivation that really matters.

When I talk about motivation, I don't mean "doing what you're told and not making waves." I think that's obedience, not motivation. I want you to aim for what we'll call **Big Mo**.

It's a term used in sports and politics to describe powerful momentum—a driving force that leads to success. Big Mo is also a good descriptor for the kind of motivation great bosses foster. When employees have Big Mo, they are:

- Self-starters
- Eager to do quality work
- Interested in solving problems
- Happy—even passionate—about their jobs, not just their paychecks

If that's the kind of employees you want, then be the kind of boss *they need*. Start by understanding the core principle of Big Mo:

Great bosses don't motivate employees—*they help employees motivate themselves.*

Think of it as the difference between *creating* and *igniting*. Managers don't invent motivation for every employee. They find out what already exists in their heads and hearts and *fuel it*. We're back to my "you can't treat everyone the same" message once again. Just as it applies to personalities, it's essential to Big Mo, so let's go. You can master this!

MOTIVATION: FROM THE OUTSIDE TO THE INSIDE

There are two categories of motivation: **extrinsic** and **intrinsic**. **Extrinsic motivators** come from outside the employee—things like salaries, bonuses, perks, and benefits.

The classic models of extrinsic motivation are piecework and commission selling. Employees are paid a fixed amount per item produced or sold. Greater productivity generates bigger paychecks. The underlying assumption is that a cash payoff will cause employees to work harder or smarter.

Books like *1001 Ways to Reward Employees* offer suggestions for other types of extrinsic motivators—things like awards and gifts for exceptional productivity, attendance, safety, or customer service.

What's not to like about extrinsic motivators? They pay our bills and they pat us on the back. And we certainly know how demotivating it can be to be grossly underpaid and to feel underappreciated. So, by all means, bosses should advocate for fair compensation and benefits for their staffers. But that's only the starting point. Money alone doesn't guarantee Big Mo.

Most of us know people who left good-paying jobs because they didn't feel fulfilled. We also know people who turned down offers of better paying employment because those jobs just didn't provide the kind of work satisfaction they crave. Something inside of them said, "I need more than this to be happy at work."

That leads us directly to **intrinsic motivation**—and why it is so important for bosses to know how to bring it to life.

INTRINSIC MOTIVATION: LADIES AND GENTLEMEN, START YOUR ENGINES

Intrinsic motivation is the internal engine that drives each of us. It's the force that propels us to go out for a run, volunteer to donate blood, solve ever-tougher sudoku puzzles, or cook our special recipe for the family gathering. Each of these activities is demanding in its own way—yet we do them willingly, even eagerly, because they provide us satisfaction.

What's the story behind that personal satisfaction? What's at the core of it? When I scan the literature on motivation or simply talk to employees, these are the high points—several internal drivers that people care about:

- **Competence:** I get enjoyment from doing things I'm good at.
- **Autonomy:** I like to have a choice and a voice in what I do.
- **Purpose:** I'm proud of having an impact and making a difference.
- **Growth:** I like moving forward—becoming smarter, better, and more accomplished.

Think about it: As you prepare that special family meal, you know your culinary *competence* is in high gear and high demand. When you go for that run, it is completely your *choice* to do it when and where you please, and for as many miles as you wish. When you give blood, you endure a little discomfort, but you do it willingly, with the higher *purpose* of helping others. And when you *grow* your skills and master the tougher sudoku puzzles, you love the brain workout and the internal voice that says, *"YES! I proved I could do it."*

If competence, autonomy, purpose, and growth drive happiness and motivation in our personal activities, it follows that they are every bit as important—perhaps even more important—in our work lives.

Now consider this: Imagine how discouraging it must be to work for bosses who are clueless about the intrinsic stuff. Instead, their approach to motivation is limited to finances, flattery, and fear—what some people call the "carrot and stick approach." They believe motivation consists of offering rewards for good work and threatening punishment for bad—and that's that.

It's possible that you've been that boss—up until now. Don't worry. Let's just tap into *your* intrinsic motivators. I know you want to build your **competence** and **grow** as a boss. I believe your **purpose** is to make a real difference as a leader. You can do this—with the **autonomy** to do it your way. I'll help with some insights and tips on how to turn competence, autonomy, purpose, and growth into Big Mo.

COMPETENCE BUILDS CONFIDENCE AND MOTIVATION

When I'm teaching about the competence motivator, I'll ask a class if anyone plays a musical instrument. There are always several. We talk about what practice was like back when they first started taking lessons. People wince, remembering that awful feeling of incompetence. They tell stories of parents cajoling them to keyboards or their self-struggle to keep strumming those guitar chords. But as their skill improved, so did their motivation to practice and perform. Once they hit competence, they were motivated to play for the fun of it. That's how it happens with work, too. We want to do more of what we're good at because it makes us happy.

Great bosses know their employees well enough to identify what they do well and what they're proud of. These managers talk to people about their strengths and why those contributions are valuable to the team. Such as this boss:

> *He leads by example and I found myself wanting to work better and harder under his guidance. He has a motivational magic that sort of oozes out of him. I think he has a talent for identifying what people are good at and/or excited about and offering them an opportunity to do what they do best. He's involved, but not micromanaging in his approach.*

That manager understands the delicate balance involved in giving people work assignments. You need to stay close enough to know them as individuals, to know what makes them tick, what they're good at, and what makes them happy. You give them sufficient opportunities to be motivated by competence, so they'll trust and accept when you ask them to take on other duties, even those that aren't their favorites. After all, we rarely get to do *only* those things we love at work (that's why they call it work, right?). But as the Gallup organization discovered in research about talented employees, one of their key motivators is their ability to say this:

> At work, I have the opportunity to do what I do best every day.

The competence motivator also explains why managers shouldn't reserve praise for only the most extraordinary performance. If you do that, you are missing a chance to reinforce your employees' good contributions by recognizing their everyday competence. Think about it: If I tell you that you're my go-to person when it comes to a particular skill, talent, or task, it's a reputation you'll work hard to maintain.

Autonomy Is Motivating—and Good for Business

If you think the essence of management is controlling the work and those who do it, you'll struggle with the concept of autonomy. You may worry that giving people more input into their work is an invitation to anarchy. But there's a business case to be made for giving employees a greater voice in the workplace. Psychologist Edward Deci is one of the preeminent voices in the study of intrinsic motivation. In his book *Why We Do What We Do: Understanding Self-Motivation*, he argues for employee autonomy and against the management inclination to control:

> Not only do controls undermine intrinsic motivation and engagement with activities but—and here is a bit of bad news for people focused on the bottom line—they have clearly detrimental effects on performance of any tasks that require creativity, conceptual understanding, or flexible problem solving.

Add to that these thoughts from author Daniel Pink's book *Drive: The Surprising Truth About What Motivates Us*:

> [R]esearchers at Cornell University studied 320 small businesses, half of which granted workers autonomy, the other half relying on top-down direction. The business that offered autonomy grew at four times the rate of the control-oriented firms and had one-third the turnover.

Why is autonomy so powerful? I've said it before. People are more likely to embrace ideas and solutions of their own creation. If we are the parent of an idea, we work harder to nurture it. That's why autonomy is such a powerful motivator.

What does it mean to be a boss who provides more autonomy to employees? You share more information. Whenever possible, you get staff input on decisions that affect them. You look for opportunities to give people more choice in designing their work, not less. You give them attention and support but you don't micromanage. Your fingerprints aren't all over their work. When there's a tie—say, you've got a good idea and so does your employee—*the tie goes to the employee.*

Here's feedback on a boss who's figured this out, from an employee who clearly appreciates him:

He has a working style that works very well for me. He is discreet, patient, considerate, doesn't raise his voice, is not pushy, is not overbearing, and has not once—ever—taken my chair and worked my computer mouse, thankfully. He keeps his cool on deadlines, focuses on tasks that need to be done, pitches in as a team player for whatever is needed, and is consistent with praise and feedback. I'll say again how much I value that he gives us the time and space to develop and try our ideas, and at the end of the process, leaves it in our hands to make the final call.

That particular boss got similar praise from other staff members. They described him as an "undoubted authority." He proves that a boss can be very much in the mix with the team, hold them to high standards, *and* play to that intrinsic motivator—autonomy—by sharing power with them.

Purpose Has Motivational Power

I think this is an area of tremendous opportunity for managers. It's related to the "vision" idea we examined back in chapter 4. How often do you remind people of the impact their work has, the good they do, and the value they bring to others? Do you tie their work to a sense of purpose?

If you're one of those "feeling" types, this may come more easily to you. Feelers are more inclined to talk about matters of the heart when it comes to work. Thinkers prefer to stick to facts rather than feelings. If you're a "thinker," let me frame it this way for you: Reminding your employees of the contributions they make to society isn't just touchy-feely flattery. It's an employee incentive that costs you nothing. Meaningfulness can be a metric that's good for business.

Please don't make the mistake of assuming work has to be heroic to be meaningful. People bring a sense of purpose and service to all manner of work—from defending our country to cleaning restrooms. The problem is, too many employees have to wait until their retirement ceremonies to hear testimonials about how the work they did affected so many others. Whose fault is that?

Managers, it doesn't cost you a dime to remind people of the meaning of what they do, especially when you catch them doing something, however small, that proves it.

Let me share a personal story to illustrate what I mean:

It's 2001. I'm at Disney World with my eleven-year-old son Mac. I've taught at a professional conference held there, and now we're off to one of the parks for some fun. Our first stop is an ice cream stand featuring our favorite: hot fudge sundaes. As we place our order, the friendly young woman behind the counter surprises us with a question: Would we like a little fudge or a lot of fudge?

Mac and I exchange grins. We can't recall *ever* using the words "little" and "fudge" in the same sentence. We opt for "a lot." We ask the server if many people actually want less, not more. You'd be surprised, she tells us. People's tastes vary, so she makes it a point to ask—and to custom-craft her sundaes.

We take our mega-chocolate treats to a shady spot and savor their perfection. I keep thinking about that server. She scoops ice cream all day. Doesn't cure cancer. Doesn't rescue people from burning buildings. Doesn't invent new technologies—although for all I know, someday she might. But at that moment, she makes sundaes *and* makes a special experience for customers, because of the extra touch she brings to her work.

As we finish up, I suggest to Mac that we go back to the stand and tell the server how much we enjoyed her masterpieces. Mac reminds me that we already thanked her when we paid. I explain my reason for wanting to say more: At the end of her shift, she'll go home. Someone may ask her about her day—and she will be able to say that her work made a mom and son so happy that they made a special trip back to salute her.

You should have seen her smile when we did.

☽

Bosses, I bet you've got your own versions of that sundae maker on your team. When was the last time you talked to them about the impact, the meaning, or the purpose of their work?

GROWTH: GETTING BETTER, STRONGER, OR SMARTER IS A MOTIVATOR

Here's another question I like to ask managers—and it's about their own motivation: I ask them to recall a time when they just couldn't wait to come to work. What was it about that task or situation that made it so motivating? They often describe something that was frightening at first:

- A project they'd never tackled before
- A big idea they'd suggested and they now had to make happen
- A critical incident that demanded the best of everyone

Then they describe how good they felt once they got past that initial fear. Learning something new, trying something different, breaking old boundaries—it revved up their internal engines.

Great bosses figure out when someone is ready for what's called a "stretch assignment." They give that employee a challenge—knowing there's risk involved to everyone if the employee fails. But the managers minimize that risk by choosing the right task, the right time, and by staying close enough to help but not to meddle.

They also know how to keep people feeling a sense of forward motion, especially when a project or task is complicated or challenging. Management expert Kenneth Thomas, in his book *Intrinsic Motivation at Work*, reminds managers of the importance of tracking and noting milestones in projects, because it gives employees a psychological boost to see concrete evidence of progress.

I especially like Thomas's take on why intrinsic motivators are so powerful:

> Basically, intrinsic rewards are those things about the work that feel good—that generate positive emotions. To harness them is to understand these emotions and to amplify them.

Here's my advice on how to amplify them in the best way. Deliver the message that fuels the "growth" motivator—and Big Mo. It's short and simple:

> I believe in you.

Time and again, when people describe great bosses, they talk about people who saw potential in them before they saw it in themselves; whose belief caused them to strive to be better and live up to that expectation.

> I believe in you.

Now, that's how *I'd* say it. You might use other words. I trust that you know your people well enough to phrase it in a way that's authentic to you and perfect for the recipient. So if it's, "Hey partner, go for it. I know you won't blow it," and that works for both of you, more power to you.

Just make sure that your way with words results in feedback that sounds like this:

He sets high expectations for us, but makes sure we know that he has complete confidence in our ability to meet the challenge.

Or:

I believe I had my largest period of professional growth in the short time she was my supervisor.

Or:

He gently moved me on to a challenge I didn't think I was really interested in, only to find that I was.

For each of these employees, growth was clearly a motivator—and their bosses knew how to rev that internal engine.

Big Mo: The Perfect Blend of Intrinsic and Extrinsic

Let's revisit that core principle of Big Mo:

Great bosses don't motivate employees—*they help employees motivate themselves.*

It happens in a two-step process: Find the engine, then add the fuel. That is, identify each employee's key *intrinsic* motivators and then apply *extrinsic* motivators to ignite them.

As a manager, you become vigilant about asking, listening, and observing so you understand those internal engines.

Then you reach into your toolkit of extrinsic motivators: information, praise, thanks, constructive criticism, coaching, mentoring, stretch assignments, titles, awards, learning opportunities, leadership opportunities, promotions, pay, perks, and more—and you apply the right ones. The plan for each person will be customized, because, as you know, you can't treat everyone alike.

To make all this easier for you, I've developed a worksheet that helps identify intrinsic and extrinsic motivators of all kinds, with twenty-five insights into work satisfaction.

I suggest you fill it out for yourself first. Then consider offering your employees or coworkers an opportunity to fill one out and share the answers with you. This isn't a quiz or an evaluation. It's a conversation starter and a tool to help you become a great boss.

WORK HAPPY: THE MOTIVATION SURVEY

On a scale of 1 to 10, please note the amount of satisfaction you derive from each of the following twenty-five work-related items. Select any number that seems right for you. Here's a rough guide:

- A response of 1 means "Barely satisfying to me at all."

- A response of 5 means "A fair amount of satisfaction."

- A response of 10 means "It's a major source of satisfaction to me."

But there's one catch: You can give a score of 9 or 10 to no more than FIVE of these items. This is intended to push you toward identifying your topmost motivators, although you may have many. You can distribute lower numbers any way you wish.

Please be candid about your responses. Some things on this list won't be especially satisfying to you—and that's just fine. Don't answer the way you think an employee *should* reply; just answer as an employee who wants to be happy and motivated at work.

Again, on a scale of 1 to 10, how much satisfaction do you derive from:

1. Being an employee who does things right _____
2. Being a pacesetting employee _____
3. Being an expert at what I do _____
4. Getting change-of-pace assignments _____
5. Getting additional training for new skills _____
6. Working independently _____
7. Feeling I have creative freedom _____
8. Doing something that helps others _____
9. Working as a member of a high-performing team _____
10. Feeling my ideas are appreciated and implemented _____
11. Knowing exactly where I stand with my boss _____
12. Being groomed for bigger things _____

(Continued)

13. Getting public recognition from my boss for good work _____

14. Getting private rather than public recognition from my boss for good work _____

15. Receiving economic incentives _____

16. Winning professional awards _____

17. Being asked to coach or teach others _____

18. Working with highly disciplined coworkers _____

19. Being held in high regard by my coworkers _____

20. Having friendships and harmony in the workplace _____

21. Leading a work group _____

22. Being asked to coach or mentor other employees _____

23. Liking my workspace, the physical plant _____

24. Having input about tools and technology _____

25. Being "in the loop" about the organization _____

WHAT'S YOUR MOTIVATION STORY?

Go back and take a look at your highest-numbered responses. What did you learn about yourself? Which items provide you the highest level of satisfaction—from your internal drivers and the external reinforcements and opportunities your bosses and coworkers provide? Which provide the least satisfaction? What's your unique recipe for Big Mo?

Write your story: To get the most out of this exercise, I recommend you take one more step. Write a one-paragraph summary of the story that emerged from your responses.

Here's what it might look like:

> I just took a survey about motivation at work. When forced to choose among a lot of options, I discovered that I get my greatest satisfaction from becoming an expert on a subject, getting change-of-pace assignments, and working with friendly, disciplined colleagues. When asked questions about rewards and recognition, I scored "public praise" pretty low. People might not have known that about me, but I'm just not comfortable in that kind of spotlight. But I did go for things like having my ideas appreciated and implemented, getting economic incentives, and being held in high regard by coworkers.

Now, how would you feel about having your employees take the survey and share their responses with you?

🌙

Some Big Mo FAQs

Whenever I teach about motivation, there's usually a robust question-and-answer exchange with managers, because it's such a complex and challenging topic. So let's do it in this book as well:

> *Q: No one ever asked me what gave me satisfaction at work and I survived. Isn't it the employees' job to please the boss, not the other way around?*

A: Interesting question. Why do you think it's an either/ or situation? You may have worked for some task-master bosses and survived, but we're aiming for employee engagement, not mere endurance. We're after Big Mo, where employees are self-starters and problem-solvers. Can we agree that when this is the case, both staffers and supervisors are satisfied?

Q: *All this motivation stuff seems fine for good employees. What about the ones who want more than they give, and don't give much?*

A: Ah, the old "balance of trade" issue. It sounds like you and those employees have completely different perceptions of how much they are contributing. This falls under the category of performance management: setting expectations, providing feedback, and holding people accountable. It's where we're heading in the next chapters, so we can build on what you've learned about motivation. But your efforts to get them moving in the right direction will be more effective if you understand motivation. If they remain poor performers and you ultimately make the tough call to replace them, then you will do so knowing you've exhausted all other options.

Q: *My staff has been complaining for a long time about our cramped and rundown workspace. I went to the mat with corporate to get some money to remodel—and finally got it. If the place looks*

*better and they're happy about that, will my people
be more motivated?*

A: Glad you asked, so I can spare you some disappointment. Things like dumpy offices or grumpy bosses are demotivators. That is, they discourage Big Mo. They bum people out and make them feel they are being treated unfairly—and that can have an impact on their performance. *But*—and this is critical—*taking away a demotivator does not automatically produce motivation.* Why? Because all you are really doing is giving people *what they believed they deserved all along.* In other words, you filled a hole, but you haven't done more than that—yet. People will like the attractive workspace and feel good that the grouchy boss is gone, but to get to Big Mo, you need to do much more than fill a hole. You need to work on the intrinsics for each individual.

*Q: Our HR department tells us employees want more
feedback than they are getting. I can see where
that connects with motivation, but I'm really busy
and can't figure out how to add that to my plate.
Suggestions?*

A: I have no doubt that you have a full plate. But I have a question for you: Is it possible that you might not feel quite competent when it comes to feedback, so you're not too motivated to jump in and try? It's a common challenge for managers, many of whom never had training in this key aspect of performance management. That's why they stick with tasks they know they do well, and that can more than fill their days.

Tell you what: I can't put more hours in your day— but I can help you become twice as good as you are right now at feedback and coaching, and show you how it can fit into that packed schedule of yours. It's all in the next chapter.

I sure hope you're motivated to turn the page.

CHAPTER 9

The Secret to Performance Management: Feedback

At some time or other, we've all heard this one. A manager is asked the secret to success, and replies:

"Hire good people and get out of their way."

On the surface, it sounds appealing, doesn't it? Unfortunately, it's terribly misleading—as bogus as those weight loss ads that claim you can take a magic pill and your pounds will melt away while you sleep. No way. Whether it's dropping weight or building a quality workforce, you won't get results without hard work.

By all means, hire good people and don't micromanage them. But never become an out-of-the-way manager. Keep in close touch, with just the right touch. That's the challenge of **performance management**.

Performance management means:

- You're constantly focused on the quality of your products and your personnel.
- You hold people accountable.
- You protect against backsliding and complacency.
- You help good employees get even better.

This is the real secret to success: **Hire good people and give them great feedback.**

Employees are hungry for feedback. I know that from those thousands of 360-degree forms I've read. Time and again, even the best managers are asked by employees to provide more feedback than they're currently sharing. The bosses are usually surprised to see such demand. It prompts them to improve their feedback—both the quantity and the quality.

You can, too. I've prepared a guide for you.

JILL'S GUIDE TO GREAT FEEDBACK

We begin with the **Great Boss's Feedback Oath**. Please raise your right hand and recite the pledge:

I, as an aspiring great boss,
Do solemnly promise all workers,
That unless I am about to undergo surgery and I'm
*   talking to my anesthesiologist,*
I will never say the following words:

"If you don't hear from me, assume you're doing a good job."

I'm on a campaign to eradicate that line from every boss's lexicon. It's the anti-feedback approach to management. Those who use the "if you don't hear from me..." subterfuge are trying to persuade employees that neglect is normal and nice. Sorry. Silence with an occasional side order of criticism doesn't qualify as feedback.

So what *is* feedback, really? Here's the way I define it:

Feedback is information with intent to influence.

That simple description says a lot. Feedback isn't just talk. *It's purposeful communication designed to have impact.* It can influence your employees' work skills and habits, their collaboration and conflict resolution, their motivation and morale. Feedback can influence the quality of your product, your people, and your work environment.

But you have to do it right.

THE BEST FEEDBACK IS:

- Intentional—It's a priority and you commit to it.
- Ongoing—You never miss an opportunity.
- Specific—It's clear and detailed.

(Continued)

- Focused on behavior—Because behavior is measurable.
- Well-timed—Sooner rather than later.
- Tailored to the individual—You can't treat everyone the same, as you know.
- About listening as well as talking—Listening sends a message: You matter.
- Delivered by a credible person—That's you, right?

When you get the hang of sharing high-quality "information with intent to influence," you'll be more successful as a boss. Here's a real-life example of a manager whose employee says she's got it down to a science:

Feedback is direct, routine, and casual. You always know that she values your skills and appreciates extra effort and routine reliability as well as flashes of inspiration. But she's equally capable of addressing work that needs to be improved in a constructive manner, and helping assess how mistakes or problems can be avoided in the future. She's able to manage employees with personalities very different from her own, from the diva to the drama queen. She's good at listening to grievances, offering solutions, and giving a pep talk when needed.

That manager has mastered several of the "great boss" skills we've already discussed. She doesn't treat everyone alike, she listens, and she can "read the room" to know when people need a shot of enthusiasm. She also makes feedback a part of her daily routine.

That's a far cry from "hire good people and get out of their way," isn't it?

To master the art of feedback, you must recognize that it is more sophisticated than a pat on the back or a kick in the butt. Think in terms of a toolkit with lots of options. I've packed one for you:

YOUR FEEDBACK TOOLKIT	
Positive Feedback	**Negative Feedback**
Information (updates or good news)	Information (no news or bad news)
Reinforcement	Clarification
Appreciation	Concern
Encouragement	Correction
Praise	Intervention
Celebration	Sanction

Scan that chart and the different varieties of feedback within. We're going to focus on both sides of that chart in this chapter and the next. To get us started, I'd like your first impressions in this quick self-assessment:

1. Which type of feedback do you deliver most often?
   _____

2. Which type do you deliver least often? _____

3. Which type are you most comfortable delivering?
   _____

4. Which type are you least comfortable delivering?
   _____

When I shared the toolkit and those questions at a workshop, it provoked an "aha" moment for one manager. He realized he was an expert at "correction," and that he provided little other feedback to his staff. Until that moment, he thought performance management consisted of catching errors and correcting people. Seeing the feedback kit's full inventory helped him discover that he was using one tool only—and to his staff, it felt like a sledgehammer.

His is not an isolated case. There are plenty of what I call "corrections officers" out there—managers who primarily focus on the negative. Here's a quote from an employee who compares that type of boss to a new and improved model:

I felt that the feedback we received from our former boss was generally negative and never focused on what we were doing well. That's what I like about this boss's style. She's constructive with it. She can tell you this works, this you need to change, and I think she's better liked because of it. It's also a good motivator because hearing what I'm doing well and the areas I need to improve in makes me want to improve my weaknesses, whereas hearing a laundry list of my mistakes is frustrating and pretty much makes me hate my job.

There's impact for you—and an important insight. Employees expect to be criticized; they just don't want it to be the only type of message they receive. You may not intend to be relentlessly negative, but you can be seen that way if you miss opportunities to put those positive tools to work. Between this chapter and the next, you'll learn the best of both.

Right now, let's sharpen the positive tools in that kit of yours.

POSITIVE FEEDBACK TOOLS AND HOW TO USE THEM

Information (Updates or Good News)

As you learned in our communication chapter, great bosses know the value of keeping people in the loop. When you tell staffers about upcoming plans or what's being discussed in meetings, you *influence* not just what they know, but their feeling of connectedness and value to the organization.

I'm not telling you to spill trade secrets, but to recognize that there's an abundance of information that may seem mundane to managers but is meaningful to employees. Don't miss an opportunity to inform.

In one company's management workshop, I led the exercise in which I ask people to identify the best communicators among their own managers. The hands-down winner was a boss who had a simple ritual. When he returned from management meetings, he shared headlines with the closest available members of his team. It wasn't a big deal, just a quick huddle. Then he asked them to spread the word, which they did. In that workplace, his team was a happy oasis of info. A little intentional briefing can go a long way. This is especially important in times of change, when people aren't just curious about what's going on in meetings, they're often anxious. You can calm them down.

Needless to say, good news is always welcome feedback. But when a boss chooses to deliver it personally, it can be doubly powerful. If you send a memo to staff announcing that your company landed a big contract or your nonprofit received a major grant, it's a good news bulletin. And what's the normal human reaction to broadcast news? It's the question, "What does this mean to me?" Smart bosses know when to combine the memo with a one-on-one conversation to personalize the information.

One other tip about delivering good news: Consider delegating that duty on occasion—but for very specific reasons. Do you have a deputy who's had to deliver too much negative feedback lately—perhaps critiques of mistakes? Is there a mid-level manager whom you'd like to build up as a leader? Being the bearer of good news can provide them an opportunity to bank up some goodwill with people. Be strategic about sharing the duty: Know when *only you* should deliver the goodies and when it's a perfect opportunity for someone else to have impact.

Reinforcement

Reinforcing feedback is straightforward information designed to turn an employee's behavior into a habit. It is particularly useful when the employee needs to improve and you observe a step in the right direction. You don't want to declare victory prematurely, but you want to acknowledge progress. You've probably heard the expression, "Catch someone doing something right and tell them." That's the case here. You're saying, "Here's what I see. Here's why it's good."

Let's say you have an otherwise good employee who's a late adopter of technology. (Never happens, right?) You see that at long last, he's stepping up. It's a perfect time to use reinforcing feedback: "I notice you signed up for the new software training. Good going. It's going to make scheduling much easier for us when you're using the system. I'll touch base Friday to see how you're doing with it."

Said negatively, that same message would be, "I see you're finally taking the new software training, so we won't have to work around you anymore. I'll be watching to make sure you don't backslide."

Both messages catch the employee doing something right. Both say the boss is paying attention. Framed positively, it's reinforcement. Framed negatively, it smacks of a reprimand. If you were the employee, which one would you rather hear?

Appreciation

The humble "thank you" is an outstanding and underrated feedback tool. You can use it for everyone—from your highest performer to those who need to raise their competence. Please don't be one of those bosses who think a paycheck should be thanks enough, or that managers shouldn't thank people for doing what they're supposed to do. Your sincere gratitude matters, especially when people see that you've gone out of your way to share it.

Consider the case of a rookie manager in one of my workshops whose colleagues had great things to say about her, including her small habit with a big impact. At the end of her shift, she simply says "good night" to people on duty, including those she doesn't supervise. Among them is a guy who works in a tech center adjacent to her workspace, and who wrote this in her feedback:

> *In my nearly thirty years in this business, no one has ever made that nice gesture of appreciation. It reassures us that yes, we are part of the team.*

Imagine that. An extra effort to say "good night" can be positive feedback, because the recipient hears it as "thanks." Are there employees in your organization who've been waiting too many years for that kind of message?

Encouragement

Encouragement reminds people of your belief in them. It can build them up when they are tired or discouraged, or when they are taking risks and trying new things. Here's a quote that shows what happens when a boss with a strong professional reputation pushes people to grow, using encouragement as a key feedback tool:

> *His high standards have served him well in his own work, and as a leader, he works to raise everyone else's bar to that level. He conveys confidence in my skills and that confidence does wonders for me. This is not easy work, and many of us struggle with self-doubt at one point or another. When he lets you know in his own quiet way that he thinks you can do it, not only that, he KNOWS*

you can do it, I can't begin to tell you the powerful positive effect it has.

I can tell you the powerful positive effect: That boss has *influenced* his employees' sense of competence. He's raised it—and we know what a motivator that is.

Encouragement is targeted cheerleading, aimed at revving up performance at just the right moment. Picture a marathon. Runners are nearing the three-quarter mark and there's a hill ahead, right around the bend. Just as they hit that spot, there's someone on the sidelines with a boom box, blasting the theme from *Rocky*. That could be you, boss.

Praise

Praise costs you nothing but can pay big dividends. You can rev it up into a power tool by delivering information, appreciation, and encouragement all in one message.

What you don't want to deliver is **drive-by praise**. That's the throwaway comment you mention in passing, as you see employees:

"Hey, nice job on that report."

It's a pleasant enough message but completely without a punch. If the staffers are skeptics, they may wonder if you really read the darn thing. But if they are like most people, they're thinking, "Really, what did you like about it?" It's unlikely they'll say that—because most folks don't want to look needy or appear to be fishing for more compliments. The conversation ends there, and so does your opportunity to really influence behavior. When you provide details about something you praise, you increase your chances of getting more of it in the future.

To power up your praise, think of the three S's: specific, sincere, and soon.

- **Specific.** Provide an example: "Nice job on that report. I especially liked the way you turned all those numbers into pie charts. You made it easy to understand at a glance."

- **Sincere.** Mean what you say. If everything you praise is "awesome" and everyone who does things right is your "superstar," you might get a reputation for being disingenuous. Your praise loses its value. Interestingly, the more specific you are in your feedback, the more it demonstrates sincerity. When people hear facts, they are less likely to smell flattery.

- **Soon.** Praise works best when it comes in close proximity to the action that earned it. The recipients see that you made a special effort to enhance the moment with a good word. That said, don't assume delayed praise isn't worth delivering, just do your best to serve it while it's hot.

Another important reminder: Never underestimate the value of a personal note.

In these days of instant digital communication, a letter or card may seem quaint. But trust me, when I ask a class of managers if anyone has saved a note of thanks or praise from a boss, hands go up across the room. Those messages mean so much that they become keepsakes. Have you made that kind of impact lately?

While I'm a big fan of specific, sincere, and sooner-rather-than-later praise, I also want to share a warning. You can do all that and still undercut the impact of your praise. There are three common ways it happens—so common that I'm highlighting them for you.

Three Ways to Sabotage Your Praise

1. **Praise with "Big But Syndrome."** You start with praise—then shift into criticism. It sounds like this:

> "You did a great job handling that angry customer, **but** you talked way too fast."

Bosses do this all the time, thinking they're being efficient and effective. Not so. Your employee hears the second part of the message far more loudly than the first. I teach managers that the word "but" erases everything that comes before it.

So, how do you combat Big But Syndrome? First, be aware of how often you lapse into it. Second, whenever possible, separate criticism from praise. Ask yourself: Is it imperative that I bring up the problem now, or could it be a separate conversation? Third, if you must address a negative alongside a positive, be transparent, detailed, and future-focused. Try substituting the word "and" for "but." Trust me, this really works. It sounds like this:

> "You did a great job handling that angry customer. You talked through his billing error in a concerned, friendly tone and came up with a solution that impressed him. That's textbook service. And one tip

for next time: If you speak a bit more slowly, you'll sound even more confident."

What did you see in that statement? Specificity, sincerity, future focus, and no Big But.

2. Praise with the sting of superiority or control. Some bosses have a knack for making their praise seem patronizing—like a reminder that they're the smartest person in the room. They applaud themselves as much as the other person:

"Good job, that's just the way I would have done it. Charming the customers was my specialty back in the day."

Or:

"See how much better things turn out when you follow my instructions? You'll get the hang of this yet."

Praise that smacks of control erodes a staffer's sense of autonomy—and that's demotivating. Here's an alternative approach: Praise and ask for a lesson from the employee. It sounds like this:

"This display looks terrific with the deep blue in the background and the logo off-center like that. How do you come up with design ideas like that?"

While delivering praise, you've made the employee the expert. And if you do this in the presence of other staffers, you've provided a teaching moment for the whole team.

3. **Praise with great big strings attached.** This is really praise as negotiation. It sounds like this:

> "You do great work. I can always count on you. Listen, we're jammed up and I need you to get these extra jobs done by tomorrow morning."

When your praise is only a prelude to pressure, it's simply a bait-and-switch tactic. Make no mistake, praise *is* intended to influence behavior, to produce more of what the person is doing well. But if you frequently use praise as an in-the-moment bargaining chip, you come off as a manipulator instead of a motivator.

This doesn't mean you can't ever praise and talk about other responsibilities in the same conversation—just be sensitive to how regularly you do it, and whether it's the primary way you praise.

There's one more positive feedback tool to go—so let's get this party started.

Celebration

Celebration is positive feedback writ large: awards, rewards, and get-togethers. It's the most public acknowledgment of achievement. This is where a boss's emotional intelligence can really pay off. Your social awareness can clue you in to what's needed, for whom, and how to deliver.

You should know your employees well enough to use celebration and recognition as the perfect extrinsic motivator to fuel their internal engines. You know when a party is just the pick-me-up people need to keep moving forward. You know which members of your team appreciate public recognition and which would prefer a quiet word from you.

If you're self-aware and know you're not adept at party planning and clever awards, you're smart enough to tap skilled deputies and staff to advise you.

Don't assume celebrations aren't worthwhile unless they're expensive. I never had a big budget for "festivities" in my time as a boss, and it only served to make us more creative in our do-it-yourself-on-a-shoestring wingdings.

When our morning and late newscasts became number one in the ratings, we celebrated by inviting the rest of the station into the newsroom for treats. The morning anchors served everyone cereal and milk. Later in the day, the evening anchors dished up ice cream. I delegated the serving duties to the anchors, and they gladly accepted, so they could thank every person on staff for their part in the success. Why no champagne for such a big victory? Expense and workplace sobriety weren't the only reasons; I wanted our message to be pride and appreciation for a job well done, but not an over-the-top declaration of indomitability.

When our team did a great job covering an especially nasty Wisconsin snowstorm, I handed out "warm socks" awards— yes, real socks, for the crews who'd braved wild wind, snow, and cold to deliver the news.

When our wonderful politics reporter returned to work after treatment for breast cancer, it was an important emotional moment for the staff. So we decided to celebrate in a style she'd know well—the big finish to a political convention. As she settled into her desk, the room burst into applause, we pulled a string, and balloons cascaded from the ceiling all around her.

At the Poynter Institute, where I now work, we have both traditional and spontaneous celebrations. Whenever a faculty member publishes a book, the full staff gathers in the library, and the author uses a large quill pen to autograph a copy for a display bookcase, then says a few words of thanks to those who helped in the effort.

Often, when our president is away on business, our fun-loving vice president will announce that he's taken over the building. He then selects a staff member—usually an unsung hero—and declares a day in his or her name, during which we all congratulate the honoree with messages and high fives.

Even in teaching, I've found opportunities that prove how much people value even silly celebratory moments. Once, on a teaching trip to Denmark, I brought along a few rolls of stickers, the kind elementary school teachers use to encourage students. They said things like, "Superstar!" "A-1!" "Great Work!" and "Keep Going!" As an icebreaker exercise at the beginning of the workshop, I explained the stickers' popularity among kids in U.S. classrooms, a concept that was foreign to my hosts. I gave a roll of stickers to these serious, smart, experienced managers (all of whom spoke English) and invited them to pick a favorite and affix it to their name badge, if they pleased. There was lots of laughter as people explained their choices. Then I gave my full supply to the group and invited them to award the goofy stickers to people who shared great ideas or did cool things throughout the week. Soon, people were sporting name badges covered with "awards." During a large group dinner midweek, a person at the conference who wasn't part of my class came up to me and asked, quite earnestly, "Excuse me, how can I win some of those stickers, too?" That three dollars' worth of paper prizes I'd brought to

Copenhagen on a whim had become, because of the group's goodwill and sense of fun, a special form of currency. It was their doing, not mine. All I did was set the table for it to happen. By the way, I've also done it in the United States, with the same fun outcome. People enjoy building a culture of celebration, especially as an accompaniment to hard work.

When you use the celebration as a true feedback tool in the workplace, your goal is to make a memory. That memory is important for the honoree, but also for your organization. It's the stuff of stories that people may tell for years to come. It's a chance to reinforce what you stand for and why quality matters. My advice: Life is short. Don't hesitate to celebrate.

Right about now, I suspect you're of two minds. One is committed to sharpening every one of those positive tools. The other is concerned, because of one very practical question: *How the heck do I find time to deliver this high-quality feedback and still get all my other work done?* It's a question I hear all the time.

Here's my answer: You can't add any more hours to the day or days to the week, but you can *upgrade* every connection you make with your staff. You can turn everyday exchanges into feedback moments. I believe you can double your feedback by following a five-step path.

How to Double Your Feedback: Five Steps

1. **Take inventory.** Think about the people who report directly to you. Ask yourself: When was the last time I had

a conversation that each of them would describe as helpful feedback? As you take that inventory, look closely for patterns in your feedback. Do you tend to pay more attention to high or low performers? Do you spend more time with certain types of employees—those you hired versus those you inherited, staffers who do jobs you once did, people who seek you out, or people you personally like?

2. Know your goals for each person. Think of this as a prescription for each person's success. What do you want more or less of from them? What habits would you like them to make or break? What would you like to make certain they don't change at all? What are your overall goals for the team's quality and innovation and how can they help contribute?

3. Know their goals, too. Knowing what you want for and from your staff members isn't sufficient. You need to know their aspirations as well. Each member of your staff has long- and short-term goals, some hopes, and probably some fears, too. You can't provide powerful feedback without understanding what's in their heads and hearts. It helps you frame your words for maximum impact.

4. Watch the work with your "feedback glasses" on. Think of feedback glasses as heightened awareness—just like that phenomenon that takes place when you buy a car and begin to notice all the others like it on the road. They were always there before, but now they're on your radar.

With feedback glasses, you're spotting opportunities more often because you're constantly on the alert for details to share. You don't look only for big mistakes to correct or massive breakthroughs to cheer, as you did before donning your feedback specs. With your new lenses, you look at everyday work and you ask yourself:

- What am I seeing in their effort today that gives me an opportunity for feedback?
- What do I observe that connects with this person's goals?
- What can I take note of, however small, that demonstrates with specificity what this person is doing well or could do better? (Yes, feedback glasses work for positive and negative feedback.)

If you don't have the best memory for details, keep a notebook handy to jot down feedback observations. Then share them as soon as possible.

5. Deputize more eyes and voices. You're a busy boss. You can't review everyone's work at all times, even if your employees would like you to. So ask for help from other managers. Tell them about your goal of doubling your feedback. Get them fitted for feedback glasses, too. Just make certain that they're on the same page as you about your standards of quality and an understanding of each person's goals. By doing this, you're not only doubling your feedback, you're building it into the culture of your organization.

Now it's time for a confession. When I first became a boss, I thought that if I focused on the positive things my staff did, I'd hardly ever need to use negative feedback. I assumed I could just catch people doing things right whenever possible, then reinforce, appreciate, and celebrate.

Boy, was I naïve.

I quickly learned that performance management doesn't

work with compliments alone. Bosses have to level with people about what's working *and* what needs work, and that demands the use of negative feedback. Supervisors have to let people know where they stand, even when the message is tough to deliver and the employee isn't enthused about the news.

It's why we call them "difficult conversations." They involve tension, conflict, and risk. But when you learn to do them effectively, the gain far outweighs the pain.

So take a deep breath, imagine you're hearing the theme from *Rocky*, and let's tackle the tough stuff next.

CHAPTER 10

You Can't Be Too Nice for a Tough Talk: Negative Feedback Is Necessary

It's time for us to have a talk. I realize we've only known each other for nine chapters, but I owe it to you to tell you this:

You need to get better at delivering negative feedback.

I'm not singling you out for criticism. You're actually in good company. Of the countless bosses I've coached, very few claim to be proficient at sharing the full spectrum of feedback—especially the tough stuff. They want to do better. In the absence of good training or a wise mentor, they learn by trial and error. Those errors can harm both employees and managers, so I want you to avoid them.

We already know that one common feedback error is to

come across as relentlessly negative. But at the other extreme—and more common than you think—is the problem of the **too-nice boss**.

These are managers who are often praised for their optimistic outlook, their encouragement and empathy, their work ethic and their team approach. But after saying all those good things, their colleagues note that they may be too darn nice for their own good—and for the team's as well.

Here's a perfect example—a quote about a boss who is admired for professional expertise and people skills. Still, an employee felt compelled to offer this advice:

> *It doesn't hurt occasionally to let people know they've screwed up big time. While laid-back and calm is good for morale, people sometimes have to be reminded that there are consequences, not for honest mistakes but for repeated sloppiness and inadequate job performance. We have some of that and from time to time you gotta get our attention, for our own good. It's a fine line between being a nice boss and being too nice.*

My goal is to make that fine line much more clear so you don't cross it. Bad things happen when you're too nice to be negative. It can be downright sinful—in seven sorry ways.

SEVEN DEADLY SINS OF THE TOO-NICE BOSS

1. Workplace problems fester as you postpone dealing with them.

2. Mediocrity (and worse) flourishes because you don't challenge underperformers.

3. Needed change is delayed as you hesitate to push people out of their comfort zones.

4. Good employees who crave constructive criticism don't get it.

5. Good employees are unfairly saddled with extra duties as you work around the weaknesses of others.

6. Bullies, bigmouths, and malcontents roam free.

7. You lose respect.

I know you don't want any of those sins on your soul—and you won't, if you realize that the kindest thing you can do is to become a little less nice. Heed the words this employee wrote about the boss:

His praise is real and not skimpy; he's a bit more reticent when it comes to criticism. I'd rather have enthusiastic measures of both.

So, by popular demand, let's develop your full inventory of negative feedback tools, starting with the most simple and moving on to the most serious.

NEGATIVE FEEDBACK
Information (no news or bad news)
Clarification
Concern
Correction
Intervention
Sanction

NEGATIVE FEEDBACK TOOLS AND HOW TO USE THEM

I'm going to break these into two classifications—lightweight and heavyweight tools.

The lightweight tools are **information**, **clarification**, and **concern.** These are the stuff of everyday interactions in the workplace. Mastering these helps prep you for the heavyweights.

Information (no news or bad news)

As we noted on the positive side, when you keep people in the loop, it tells them they matter to you. If you withhold info, by accident or by design, *no news* becomes a negative feedback tool.

Staffers even pay attention to the order in which people are informed. You can cause employees to feel more—or less—valued by the timing of a message. (As in, "Why am I the last to find out these things?")

Should you withhold or delay information as a way of sending a negative message to an employee? I wouldn't advocate that. It's a passive-aggressive way of dealing with what should be a direct conversation. If you want someone to know they need to improve, say so. Don't expect them to deduce it from the fact that you've left them off a memo or didn't invite them to a meeting.

Using the "silent treatment" as negative feedback carries another danger. If you have a reputation for shutting down communication when you are displeased with someone, you run the risk of having innocent folks misread your quiet moments. On the day you're battling a nasty headache and say little to someone in the lunchroom, that person will inevitably see your Evil Twin, the Boss Who Has It In for Me.

In addition to *no news*, there's the negative feedback of *bad news*. I'm talking about common and unpopular events that happen in the world of work. It could be the resignation of a respected employee who's taking a good job elsewhere. It's not a tragedy, but events like that have the potential to shake up staff morale. It may be the announcement of a salary and hiring freeze, which hits people in the pocketbook and may cause them additional work.

When you have to deliver bad news, the best method involves realism and optimism.

- Tell the truth.
- Acknowledge the pain.
- Encourage people to see beyond the setback.

It would sound like this in the "coworker jumping ship" case:

"Rosalie is taking a job that's just too good for her to pass up. It's a big loss for us, no doubt. But it's what happens when people do excellent work and follow their dreams. Just know that I have faith in our team, and I'm counting on your talent to lead us forward."

For the wage and hiring freeze, it might sound like this:

"I've got news none of us will be happy about. Starting immediately, there's a company-wide freeze on salaries and on new hires. It's because of the economy and the business forecast for the rest of the year. I know this is disappointing and it puts pressure on all of us. I'll do my best to watch over all of our workloads. We'll be creative about solutions to any challenges that come up. I'm here for anyone who wants to ask questions or kick around ideas. We'll get through this."

Also remember that with bad news, perhaps even more than good, people want to know what it means to them individually. If you've delivered news like this to a group, some people will ask direct questions, others will hang back. Plan on having one-on-one follow-up talks with people after any group conversations. That's where your real connections happen. Be truthful and tactful.

Clarification

You might be surprised to see "clarification" listed as a negative form of feedback. I include it not because clarification is critical on its face—but because of its potential to be misunderstood when it comes from a powerful person like a boss. Asking for clarification can seem innocent enough to you, but the other person can easily take it as a criticism. It's an Evil Twin scenario, in which Curious Boss is seen as Critical Boss.

Here are some examples of how it plays out:

You Say This	They May Hear This
"I'm not clear what you meant in this email. What exactly do you need?"	"You're a lousy communicator. I'm frustrated."
"Didn't you tell me you were taking Monday, not Tuesday, as a vacation day?"	"You messed up."
"How far have you gotten on that report?"	"Why isn't it done yet?"

You thought your clarification questions were perfectly benign, boss. But somehow they came across as negative.

How does that happen?

Psychologists describe it as an error of attribution. Here's what that means: We all tend to be amateur psychologists, trying to figure out the motives behind other people's actions. The problem is that we're not very good at it. For example, let's say you're walking down the hallway at work and a top executive passes you. She says nothing in response to your friendly hello and keeps on walking. You immediately wonder why she intentionally ignored you. You're not as likely to assume she might be on her way to a budget meeting, distracted because she's crunching numbers in her head—even though that's precisely the case. We often see situations through the prism of our worst fears—and attribute the wrong motives to innocent events. It's especially the case when the other person is more powerful and whose job it is to assess our performance—like a boss.

So, in the case of clarifications, if I'm the manager who's asking the question, I *know* my motive—to clear up my confusion. I know I don't intend to be critical. But you *imagine* my motive and assume it's to find fault with you. That's even more likely to happen if an employee has low self-confidence in general.

The best way to keep clarification from coming across negatively is to recognize how easily people can mishear you. Anticipate it and communicate in a positive way. So, let's revisit those clarifications.

"Can you help me with your email message? Tell me a little more about what you need so we're both on the same page."

"This isn't a criticism, I'm just checking my memory. Didn't you say you were taking Monday instead of Tuesday off?"

"I don't know how much time you've had to work on the report, but I'm just checking in to see where it stands. Everything going okay?"

You don't have to become paranoid about this, just aware. Be doubly aware if you are communicating via email, which, as we pointed out in chapter 5, can be tone-deaf.

And, in the interest of keeping you from becoming a too-nice boss, let me just note that if you have to ask the same person for clarifications fairly often, it's probably time for you to raise it as a concern.

Concern

Concern is negative feedback at a fairly low level of threat to the employee, but it is nonetheless critical of performance. Your goal is to identify an honest error so it won't happen again, or call out a behavior before it turns into a bad habit. It's the stuff of everyday conversations in the workplace that help employees improve without making them feel like total screwups.

When you are expressing a concern, your emotional intelligence skills should guide your choice of tone. Friendly but serious usually works fine as you:

- Describe the behavior
- Explain its impact
- State the change you expect

So let's say you have a person who consistently sends you confusing emails. He's a good employee in other respects. You just want to raise the issue so he'll be more careful:

"David, I want to touch base with you about emails. For some reason, the ones you send me often skip some important information—like the contact info for the vendor, or the date of the meeting you want to set up. Here's a couple from the past few weeks. You can see that it's happening pretty often. I think you should do a read-through on your messages before hitting send. Double-check them.

That way you won't cause me extra work trying to hunt for missing info. I know that's the last thing you want to do."

Concern conversations differ from more serious discussions in a key way:

You aren't directly threatening people with discipline. You're asking them not to disappoint you.

Think back to the Power Grid. You're tapping your *referent* power rather than your *coercive*. When the staff trusts and respects you, they don't want to let you down.

Great bosses know how to wield the concern tool very effectively. It's often negative feedback framed positively: "I know you're better than this. And now that you know what you need to do differently, I have confidence you'll do it."

Here's a real-life example of a boss who knows how to express concern:

He's good at giving feedback. He's also very direct when giving criticism. On occasion, when I've messed up, his tone is one of counsel, like, "I'm surprised you missed this; what happened?"—as opposed to jumping all over me. Every error, to him, is a learning experience for the person involved.

When employees characterize your negative feedback as *their learning experience*, you know you're doing something right.

You'd also like them to feel that way when you use the heavyweight negative feedback tools of **correction, inter-**

vention, and **sanction**. But that can be a challenge, depending on the problem and the person you're addressing.

Welcome to the land of difficult conversations.

Let's quickly review each of the heavyweight tools and look at ten steps you must take when you have these tough talks.

Correction

Correction feedback is a step more serious than concern. Conversations about correction are straightforward messages to employees that say, "You must improve"—and not just because failure to do so will disappoint you, the boss. The stakes are higher.

In a correction conversation, you are telling an employee about underperformance that, while not egregious, is unacceptable. It causes extra work for other people, or doesn't follow established procedures, or adds costs or delays. That's why it must improve. You want the employee to succeed because doing any less could have negative consequences for that person's career. So, while these elements are the same as in your concern feedback:

- Describe the behavior
- Explain its impact
- State the change you expect

You must also:

- Discuss the part you'll play in helping the person improve
- Include a reality check about potential consequences of failure

Let me emphasize that last point. Unless you include a reality check about potential consequences, the employee might think you're just expressing a concern or offering some friendly advice. This is more serious.

That said, correction conversations can have happy endings. Many of them do. That's most likely to happen when the employee is committed to improving and you, the boss, aren't just a corrections officer; you're a coach. (Don't panic. I'll teach you about coaching in the next chapter.)

Most organizations require managers to document their correction conversations. Documentation is a written summary of the problem, what transpired in the conversation, and what's expected of the employee in the future. It is shared with the employee and becomes a part of that person's employment file. When you "write someone up," you should provide clear details, free of bias or rancor, so it's as objective a summary as possible.

That's especially important, because when correction conversations fail to produce the desired results, it's time for the next level up in serious negative feedback—the intervention.

Intervention

Interventions happen when the mistakes are bigger, the behavior is badder, or when, despite concern and corrective feedback from the boss, an employee hasn't improved.

Intervention conversations also involve formal documentation and usually include a clearly outlined performance improvement plan. The written plan spells out specific goals that the employee must meet, on a fixed timetable. The plan is clear about how improvement will be measured and what the consequences will be if it fails to happen.

Intervention conversations are often done with an additional person in the room—a person from Human Resources, another manager, or even your own boss. The extra person isn't there to pile on. Sometimes they say nothing at all, but their presence underscores the seriousness of the situation and they serve as a witness in case there's a dispute about what was said and by whom.

As the person delivering this highly negative feedback, you must be crystal clear in your message. You are doing this so that the employee has a last opportunity to turn things around. It's all mapped out, with everyone's responsibilities laid out in detail. It's up to the employee to choose the right path.

Sanction

This is the most serious level of negative feedback. These are conversations that inform employees about demotions, suspensions, or terminations. When the news is the worst—as a firing is—you must be at your professional best: civil, compassionate, and concise.

The person you are letting go may have failed your team in a big way, may have sniped at you before (and now), and may challenge the fairness of the action or the quality of the organization. Resist the urge to get the last nasty word. The person is leaving. You are staying. That's enough.

Remember that even though you sanction an employee in private, the news inevitably reverberates across your entire team. Let it be a message about the standards and values you stand for.

Because these three forms of negative feedback are so important, I've prepared a step-by-step method for doing them well.

Difficult Conversations: Ten Steps to Make Them Easier

1. **Know your goal.** Know exactly what you want to accomplish in the conversation. Whenever I work with bosses on difficult conversations, I find that this can be their challenge. They can rattle off a litany of things that the employee is doing wrong but they can't focus it into a goal. It sounds something like this:

> "I have this employee who's making lots of mistakes, but he blames others. He says it's the equipment or he got bad instructions or he's on a crummy shift where the workload is too heavy. He's a big complainer about management. Coworkers say his sarcasm gets on their nerves. I've talked to him about the mistakes, but pretty informally. I need to have the formal sit-down that finally gets his attention."

That's when I ask: What's your goal for this employee? When the conversation is over, **what will the employee know he must do and what will the next steps be?**

My questions force the manager to clear through the clutter and focus on the core issue. In this case, it's the employee's **mistakes**. They are measurable and they pose the greatest threat to the team.

So, the goal for the employee is: **Stop making so many mistakes**. That leads you to the goals for the conversation:

- To inform the employee about the unacceptable level of mistakes he makes, detailing what they are and the harm they cause.
- To counter his excuse making by documenting the quality of his equipment, instructions, and workload.
- To let him know you will monitor his progress with specific check-in points.
- To be clear that if he can't or won't improve, his employment status will be affected, perhaps even terminated.

I strongly encourage you to do the "what's my goal for this person and this conversation" check before every tough talk. And unless you are dealing with an ax murderer, I always suggest you include "preserve the dignity of the other person" as part of your overall goal.

2. **Know yourself.** This is where your self-awareness and self-management skills come into play in a big way. It's important to recognize your "default" approach to conflict. Some of us see conflict as a war to be won at all costs, some see it as a search for common ground, some approach it as give-and-take, while others view it as a danger to avoid.

When you know, for example, that you start from a "win this war" approach, you may turn the conversation into a prolonged argument, rather than steady, measured communication about expectations. You need to remind yourself to stay focused on your goal, not in making the other person say, "You're absolutely right. I'm completely wrong. You win."

At the other extreme, when you know you hate conflict because it makes people unhappy, you need to manage the anxiety you feel before, during, and after a tough conversation. You can do that by reminding yourself that you aren't helping employees by shielding them from negative feedback. Worse, you're hurting the rest of the team by your reluctance to address underperformers.

3. **Prepare.** Have your bases covered before you launch your difficult conversation.

- **Gather information.** The more serious the issue under discussion, the more you need examples and documentation. Whether in praise or criticism, details provide credibility. The more challenging the conversation, the more you might even consider rehearsing it with another manager in advance. It can help you avoid surprises.

- **Look up.** Your boss has a stake in your difficult conversations. In most cases, your boss expects you to deal with the everyday feedback automatically and on your own. But each boss also has an "involve me" threshold that you should clearly understand. Know when your boss expects you to consult before a conversation or advise afterward. The more challenging the conversation, the more you want to go into it knowing your supervisor has your back. Make certain your boss agrees with your assessment of a situation and the appropriate response.

4. **Start strong.** This is another time when opening lines set the tone for the whole talk. You choose them based on the nature of the problem. The more serious the situation, the more direct you should be about the bad news. A less serious or more sensitive topic may call for another approach.

For example, you don't open a conversation about an employee's chronic body odor problem the same way you inform an employee that he's fired.

Okay, I know you want to see examples of both openers, so I'll oblige. In each case, remember your goals.

For the hygiene conversation, your goal is to get the employee to take the necessary steps to eliminate the odor. While addressing the problem honestly, you want to minimize the inevitable humiliation factor about something so personal. Since this one seems to be a real favorite in my seminars (what is it about B.O.?), I'll share both sides of the conversation and how it could play out:

YOU: Hi, come on in. How's it going?

STINKY: Pretty good. We've been busy because it's vacation season and we're down a couple of people.

YOU: I understand. Do you have vacation plans?

STINKY: I'm taking time in October for my sister's wedding.

YOU: Nice time for a wedding. We held ours in fall, too. Listen, before I start boring you with my wedding stories, I want to talk with you about work. There's something I think you probably don't know about—but I owe it to you to let you know.

STINKY: What? What's up?

YOU: Well, this may be embarrassing to hear, but I need to let you know that from time to time, your deodorant must be failing you. When that happens, I'm afraid you have noticeable body odor here at work.

STINKY: Are you kidding? Who's complaining about me? Who's saying this?

YOU: I'm saying this. Just like I'd hope you'd tell me— so I could do something about it. That's what this is about—getting it taken care of. Let's talk about what you can do.

My start was slow and positive, consistent with the goal of minimizing humiliation while introducing the negative news and getting the employee to address it.

Now consider the firing conversation. You have an employee who has failed to meet the minimum standards you laid out in a six-month plan for improvement, and the time has come to part ways. Your conversation begins this way:

YOU: Marci, I want to be up-front about the reason we're here. The purpose of this meeting is to tell you we are letting you go. We have information for you from Human Resources about the next steps and to answer any other questions you might have.

Yes, it is just that direct. Don't make the mistake of burying the bad news. If you begin by chronicling the history of the past six months—complete with the conversations and the disappointing outcomes—you may think you are justifying the bad news, but you are actually tormenting the person. Your long introduction may suggest that you're open to a discussion or negotiation when that's simply not going to happen. You're delaying the inevitable and that's neither kind nor fair. (And by the way, I hope your firing conversations will be humane—and rare.)

5. Don't pile on. Some bosses, especially those who put off tough talks, compile a private list of grievances about a staffer. They carry it in their heads, letting it bug the heck out of them—while not dealing with it. Then, when a significant enough problem finally triggers a conversation, the manager unloads everything—from the important to the petty. The boss's appropriate goal of solving a key problem gets obscured in that barrage of criticism. Don't purge; focus on what really matters. More important, make a habit of tackling issues early—when they're small. Not only won't you have things to pile on, you may actually keep small issues from becoming significant.

6. Focus on behaviors. In any situation involving negative feedback, focus your words on behaviors, not your assumptions about that person's character or motives. There's a big difference between telling an employee "You're late" and "You're lazy." Lateness is a behavior you can document; laziness is a subjective judgment, much harder to prove and quite possibly wrong. In addition, making it personal automatically triggers the other person's defenses.

Compare these two different ways of addressing a person who's let you down:

"When you don't respond to email requests, which happened three times this week, it causes delays in our decision-making."

Or:

"It's so unprofessional of you to think it's okay to ignore emails."

As I always tell managers, you don't know what people *think*. You know what they *do*. The second message got personal, made assumptions, and invited a defensive reply. The first stated facts. It didn't call names or presume to know what the person was thinking. Don't attack people, address problems. Focus on behaviors and their impact.

7. **Expect emotion.** Emotion—yours and theirs—is a normal part of conflict and difficult conversations. Make certain you manage yours well.

• **Avoid hyperbolic language.** If you overstate your case, you undercut your credibility. It sounds something like this:

"You always claim someone else is at fault, you never double-check your work, nobody else makes this many errors, and everyone here is upset about it."

Hyperbolic rhetoric sets you up for possible challenge—or correction. When you're tempted to use inflated language, ask yourself: Would I really want to have to document these words—or eat them?

• **Anticipate tears.** They happen. Pause to let the other person regain composure. Don't assume, as one tough boss told me, that employees cry just to manipulate you. It's reflexive with some people. Keep tissues handy.

• **Don't fight fire with fire—or gasoline.** If the other person starts to shout or swear, you have a choice. You can keep control of the situation or you can lose it. It takes courage to keep cool when the other person is combative or profane. But remember: Just because you don't respond in kind, it doesn't mean you are backing down. You are being strategically resolute. You are thinking more clearly because you are calm and keeping the upper hand because you are composed.

And then there's one more practical advantage to minding your temper and your language. If the other person's outburst is sufficiently over-the-top that you must report it to Human Resources for possible disciplinary action, the folks there will want to know every detail of what happened. You don't want them saying to you, "You said *what*? Those words? You just tied our hands."

8. Stay on track. Don't let a difficult conversation become a debate, even if you're a person who loves a good argument. Here's how it can happen. You bring up a performance issue and the employee replies:

"What about Steve? He does the same thing and you never call him on it!"

Or:

"We have much bigger problems than this—what about our equipment failures?"

I call those responses "deflections." They happen all the time in difficult conversations. People want to shift the focus from themselves so they toss out peripheral issues—and you might just take the bait and debate, just to prove you're smart, and right.

Don't fall for the trap. Direct the conversation back to the main issue. Let's revisit and respond to those deflections:

Deflection: What about Steve? He does the same thing and you never call him on it!
Response: I want to talk about your situation, because that's what's important. And just as you wouldn't appreciate me talking about you with other staffers, we won't make this a conversation about Steve. Here's the situation...

And:

Deflection: We have much bigger problems than this—what about our equipment failures?
Response: I know you have strong feelings about equipment quality. That's not where we're going today. I want us to stay focused on you.

Remember, when they deflect, you redirect—and don't debate.

9. **End smart.** When it's time to end the conversation, a summary is a great wrap-up. It provides one last opportunity for you to restate your key goals and to make sure everyone is on the same page. Remember, people don't hear well when their emotions are engaged, so it's your last chance for clarity.

- Here's what I said and what I heard you say.
- What did you hear from me?
- Here's what happens next.

10. **Follow up.** When you deliver negative feedback, always think about next steps. For bigger issues, it may be a memo summarizing what was agreed upon or a check-in meeting to assess progress. It's equally important to follow up in some way after a minor correction. Employees often hang on to the anxiety of a difficult conversation, thinking they've lost standing in your eyes. In a case of a minor correction, your follow-up might just be a brief and pleasant chat about work, something that lets the employee know he or she is not being viewed by you in a continuing negative light.

☾

Congratulations, you're now well versed in the finer points of feedback, both negative and positive. But to really boost employee performance, you need to add one more tool to your cool new kit: *You have to learn to coach.*

Here's the bonus: It will make your job easier. I promise.

CHAPTER 11

Stop Fixing, Start Coaching

I could sing the praises of bosses who know how to coach, but nothing says it better than a grateful employee:

She has been a wonderful coach, both directly and indirectly. When I go to her to ask for advice, she guides me in such a way that I am instilled with insight and confidence to make the decision myself.

That boss is on to something really important: teaching people how to make their own good decisions, instead of just telling them what to do. Coaches do that—and more. Bosses who coach can raise the quality of work, workers, and the workplace. Coaching is feedback on steroids. But here's what I've discovered among the many managers I've encountered:

There are too few coaches and too many fixers.

Fixers aren't bad bosses, mind you. They are responsible managers who care about quality, but they do far more telling than teaching. If there were a Fixer's Creed, it would be this:

Bring me your problems and I will give you solutions. Show me your work and I will improve it, even if it means doing it for you. It's my duty as a boss.

Fixers get the job done, but through micromanagement and control. Coaches learn to let go of all that and achieve even better results. How do I know? As I tell the managers in my workshops:

"I stand before you as a recovering fixer. If I could learn to be a coach, so can you."

Let the coaching lesson begin—with **questions**. As you'll soon learn, questions are a coach's best friend.

FIVE QUESTIONS ABOUT COACHING

1. What exactly is coaching?
   Coaching is *guided discovery*. You're the guide. The other person discovers.

2. What can I use coaching for?
   A coach helps someone make a decision, solve a problem, or improve a skill.

3. Why is coaching so effective?
   Coaches don't tell people what to do—or do it for them. They help people figure out answers for themselves. After all, people like their own ideas best. They're more committed to them because they give birth to them. The coach is just the midwife.

4. What's a coach's most important tool?
   The question. (Thanks for asking!)

5. What's so important about questions?
   By asking the right questions, a coach triggers the other person's thinking. The coach's questions are carefully chosen to help the other person see possibilities that might not be obvious to them.

I suspect you're thinking, "Nice theory—but what does it look like in practice?" I'll show you. We'll use a case study that represents the kind of coaching I do with managers all the time. Please pay attention to the use of questions.

A COACHING CASE STUDY: JIM AND THE ERROR-PRONE ALSO-RAN

The Situation: Jim is a manager who wants some guidance. He is concerned about a decline in the quality of an employee's work. He says the employee has gotten sloppy, making more errors than usual. Jim wants to figure out the best way to approach the employee about the problem. Then Jim adds, "I should point out that he applied for the same management job I did. I think he's still mad that I'm the one who got it. What do you think I should do?"

As a coach, I resist my old fixer ways. Fixers tend to give quick answers. They pass judgment on the situation and tell the person what to do. In this case, a fixer might say:

"Well, it's time for your employee to get over the past and focus on performance. If he's mad at the situation, he shouldn't take it out on his work or on you. You need to deal with the problem, so call him in and focus on the sloppiness. If they're not big errors, don't make a big deal but get it all out on the table. Here's what you could say..."

Or perhaps this:

"I think you should just leave the promotion stuff aside. He might be over it by now. When I was promoted I had a similar situation. I could tell you stories about that. Anyway, in my opinion, you just have to let that go. Find out what's going on with the mistakes. Get examples of his work and show him."

The conversation would go on for a while and it would very likely include questions—*But the questions would be coming from Jim, the answers from the fixer.* That's the customary fixer format: You ask, I tell. Jim will move forward, but he's acting largely on my ideas, not his own.

What a Coach Would Do

Now let's see how a coaching conversation would play out by comparison.

The coach listens to Jim and, like the fixer, has some gut feelings about the situation. But the coach uses questions to plumb for more information as well as potential solutions.

COACH: So, he's making more errors than usual. What kind of errors?

JIM: He transposed some numbers on one document and we had to redo an invoice. He also forgot to process some paperwork two weeks ago. Last week I sent him an email request for some figures and it took him three days to get back to me. It's like he's off his game.

COACH: So you're concerned this might be a trend, but you haven't talked to him about that yet. You also said you think he might have hard feelings about not getting the promotion. How recent was your promotion?

JIM: Five months ago.

COACH: What makes you think he's angry about it now?

JIM: He told someone he was ticked off because he had a few more years' experience than me but I got the job.

COACH: So you heard it through the grapevine. When was that?

JIM: Back when the promotion was announced.

COACH: And when you talked with him about it, what did he say?

JIM: I didn't pursue it with him because I only heard it indirectly.

COACH: Interesting how those things can stick in your mind, though, isn't it? How often do you talk with him about work in general or about his performance, bad or good?

JIM: Probably less than I should. He's pretty self-sufficient. But I see where you're coming from.

COACH: What do you mean?

JIM: Maybe I should have been talking with him more. I just didn't want to act like I was lording it over him, so I hung back. We've started using a new software program—maybe he's having trouble with it.

COACH: That could be. Any other possibilities?

JIM: We're in vacation season and shorthanded. Maybe it's a workload issue. I'll just take him aside for a check-in. I'll ask about the software. I can use that as a way to get into the mistakes. I've got a printout from last week so I can show him.

COACH: Sounds like you want to get the issues on the record but not have him feel beaten up, especially since it's the first conversation you've had in a while. How do you think he'll respond?

JIM: I think he'll be okay. He's not a hothead. I can even ask for his input on the new project we're launching, too. I can make this work.

I have coaching conversations like this all the time. Instead of immediately telling the person what *I think* and what they should do, I listen, analyze, and craft my questions accordingly. Sometimes I help people broaden their focus, other times I help them narrow it. My goal is that they *tell me the answers they're coming up with.*

Here's the cool part: Their answers are usually better than the ones I would have offered right out of the blocks as a fixer. Why? Because *by asking good questions*, I almost always surface some additional information or context, which leads to a better decision-making. Best of all, it's *their* decision. They've named it and claimed it.

Now think about the benefits of doing this as a boss. You're upgrading the quality of your feedback. Implicit in a coaching talk is the message: *I trust that you can figure this out.*

Power Up Your Questions

Coaching is built on questions—but they have to be good ones. The most powerful coaching questions are:

- **Clear and direct.** Notice that I didn't make my questions complicated or meandering. They aren't designed to be a lecture or a quiz. They're designed to clarify a situation and lead people to a solution.

- **Open-ended**. That means they can't be answered with just a yes or a no. They require the respondent to think and add more information. "What kind of errors?" "What makes you think that?" "What do you mean?" "Any other possibilities?" Use closed-ended questions if you want to gather facts, open-ended questions if you want to open up options and mine for ideas.

- **Nonjudgmental.** They're not loaded with criticism. I didn't ask, "Why the heck have you held off talking with him?" or "Isn't it foolish to keep worrying about something you heard secondhand five months ago?" I didn't have to. My combination of open-ended and closed-ended questions led Jim to decide he may have been wasting some time and worry.

- **Sometimes provocative—for a purpose.** Being nonjudgmental doesn't mean you can't nudge the person a bit. Notice my question to Jim: "What did he say when you talked with him about it?" I suspected that he hadn't, because it's the kind of tough talk so many managers avoid. My "when you talked with him" framing is a nonthreatening way of telegraphing that Jim could have cleared the air before now. It led Jim to acknowledge his own inaction. I didn't criticize him. He took care of that himself.

As you can see, good questions lead to *guided discovery*.

MY TOP TEN COACHING QUESTIONS

As you become more of a coach than a fixer, you'll develop your own inventory of questions that work well for you. In the meantime, let me share some that I have found to be very effective. I've already told you about "What did the person say when you discussed it?"—which I encourage you to use regularly, because I've seen it work! Here are some of my other favorites:

1. **How can I help you?** It's a friendly opening line—with a purpose. It's designed to get people to state their goal at the very start of the conversation. Too often, people say, "Can I run something past you?" and launch a long story while you figure out where this is all going. "How can I help you?" leads them to give you a headline in advance. It can expedite the process.

2. **What's the worst that could happen?** This question works when you are coaching people who lack self-confidence or are sensitive about risks. Getting them to state their worst fears enables you to follow up with questions about how realistic their fears may be—like this: "You said you're worried that Sam might quit if you give him these new responsibilities but no raise. What are you basing that on? How bad would it be if it really happened? What alternatives do you have?" The "worst case" question can actually free people to talk about what they thought was unspeakable.

3. **Can you tell me more about how you know this?** I use this one when people seem convinced there's only one reason something is the way it is. It's a great way to find out whether they are operating on faulty facts (rumors, assumptions, old information) or have put blinders on and aren't looking for other possibilities. It inevitably opens the door for more questions—and insights.

4. **What does this person do well?** This is a question I've learned to ask when bosses are describing a problematic employee. After I've heard a litany of all the person's weaknesses, I ask, "What does this person do well?" It's often an amazing game-changer, especially when the manager has avoided a difficult conversation for a long time, while collecting a list of grievances. Asking this question helps me determine

whether the boss (rightly or wrongly) has written off the employee as irredeemable—or wants to salvage the situation.

5. **Knowing what you know now, would you hire this person today?** This is definitely a closed-ended question—designed to elicit a yes or no answer. I ask it when managers are struggling with decisions about employees who are mediocre or have a jumble of strengths and weaknesses—but don't improve, despite the boss's best efforts. The question, "Knowing what you know now, would you hire this person?" can lead to less emotional and more rational decision-making.

6. **Who else has a stake in this?** Asking this question is a nonjudgmental way of reminding people that it's not all about them. It prods them to look in all directions around an issue to see how it affects others. Identifying other stakeholders is one of the most important things a coach can do. It can also lead to the next valuable question:

7. **Who could be your allies in this?** I'm a big believer in encouraging people not to go it alone. Asking them to enlist allies challenges them to collaborate with others—who can both help them meet their goals and also hold them accountable.

8. **What happens if you do nothing?** This question can serve as a call to action—or inaction. Their answer may describe how difficult things will be if they fail to act, and push them to finally do what they've been avoiding. On the other hand, if they have overstated a problem or are worrying needlessly, their answer can lead them to recognize that the status quo may be just fine.

9. **So, what's success going to look like?** Think back to our friend Jim in my coaching conversation. This is a question I would ask him as we wrap up. It's an upbeat question, which sets a positive tone. It's also my last chance to hear him

spell out his goal—which might have shifted a bit during the coaching, as is often the case. We agree on what he plans to accomplish and how he will measure whether he's achieved it. It's a push for specificity.

10. **What are your next steps?** This is a good closer. It can turn goals into plans and plans into action. It's a check to see if the person I'm coaching is going to follow through. If a solution is somewhat challenging or complex, it chunks it down into a series of smaller, defined actions. It gives me one last opportunity to make certain that a person I've coached is better off than when our conversation began!

IMPORTANT COACHING REMINDERS: EARS, EYES, AND VOICE

Coaches need to be really good listeners, fully focused on the other person. You're tuned into what people say, how they are saying it—and what they're *not* saying. The quality of your listening improves the quality of your questions. Remember the listening tips from chapter 5:

- Make eye contact—no distractions.
- Check your body language—oriented toward the person, open and friendly.
- Repeat key ideas—to make sure you've heard accurately and they know you're tuned in.

Tone matters, too. As you ask your questions, don't forget the tone of your voice. The best questions will lose their effectiveness if they come across as condescending or chastising—or as a police interrogation.

Remember, your goal is to guide people to discover their own answers. In the process, they often realize they've been wrong about something. As a coach, you're not trying to embarrass them further. It's very common that after you help a person come up with a new approach to an old problem, he or she will say:

"I feel pretty stupid that I hadn't figured this out until now."

This is your chance to give the one-time coaching event a longer-term payoff. It can come in the form of encouragement and—you guessed it—a question:

"Don't get down on yourself. You figured it out and that's what counts. What's the takeaway for the future for you?"

I'm sure you know why that question is important. The best coaches try to put themselves out of business. The better your employees' decision-making, the less guidance they need from you. You are building a stronger, smarter, and more independent workforce.

What If I Have Some Skeptical Questions About Coaching?

That's fine with me. Fire away!

> *Q: I'm busy enough as it is. Isn't coaching going to take a lot of time?*

A: Only if you let it or if you're not good at it. I suggest you go back and read Jim's case study aloud—and time it. A talk like that could take less than five minutes, the same amount of time as a comparable fixer conversation in which Jim asked a series of questions and the fixer gave answers. Don't worry: coaching involves analysis and questions, but not psychoanalysis. You can do it on the fly, in the midst of a busy day. You don't need a couch to be a coach.

Q: *Aren't there times a boss should ditch the coaching questions and just tell the person what to do?*

A: Yes, absolutely. Park your questions and give instructions when a situation is urgent and speed is essential, when you are asked about a judgment call that only a boss should make, or when you have a genuine belief that a particular person will benefit from direct instructions this time. (Remember, you can't treat everyone the same, right? Even in coaching.) This still leaves an abundance of opportunities for coaching every day.

Q: *What if people just want answers and not questions?*

A: It's your job to figure out whether that's a good or a bad thing. If you're a coach who's developed a smart team of independent decision-makers, they'll come to you for answers because they've already done their best to think them through—and now they want your two cents, for good measure. Answer away!

But if you're a fixer, you've probably trained them to rely on you for answers instead of coming up with their own. I think some of the most dangerous words you can hear from employees are these:

"Just tell me what you want me to do."

It means your employees lack the skill, the will or the permission from you to take initiatives themselves. In that case, it's time to ask *yourself* a question: "Am I causing this?"

Do you want to find out how much of a micromanager or fixer you might be? I've put together a short questionnaire so you can evaluate yourself.

CHECK YOURSELF: THE MICROMANAGEMENT ASSESSMENT—ARE YOU A FIXER?

Answer these questions, using a scale of 1 to 10, with 10 meaning, "Yes, absolutely."

1. I delegate everyday decision-making to the people closest to the work. _____

2. I've made sure my staff knows the point at which an issue requires my input, and they see that threshold as reasonable. _____

3. I know how to ask good questions so people come up with their own solutions. _____

4. When I share my expertise with employees, I try to teach them *how* to do something rather than telling them *what* to do. _____

5. I don't do or redo people's work for them to make it better, instead I coach them to improve it themselves. _____

6. When I keep a hand in the work of the team, I help in ways they appreciate. _____

7. If I closely supervise employees because their work needs improvement, I give them clear feedback on their performance so they know why I'm involved. _____

8. I enjoy giving people increasingly greater responsibility and authority as they grow. _____

9. Even when I'm under pressure from my own bosses, I try not to become a dictator to my team. _____

10. I would hate to be known as a micromanaging fixer. _____

Your total score: _____

If your score is below 80, chances are you've been brutally honest with yourself, and you now know you've been more of a fixer than a coach. Which of the questions brought down your score? That's where your self-improvement work should begin. Just like mine had to.

As I've already confessed: I'm a recovering fixer.

If I had taken that assessment years ago, I think my score would have been in the low 70s, largely because I didn't know how to ask coaching questions and I didn't delegate well, but most of all because I would have flunked this question:

> I don't do or redo people's work for them to make it better, instead I coach them to improve it themselves. _____

My honest (and painful) self-score on that one would have been a big fat ZERO.

Since I teach from my mistakes to keep others from repeating them, I'll tell you the embarrassing story of my wake-up call.

How I Learned to Sit on My Hands (and Become a Coach)

It was the early 1990s and I was one happy TV news director. I had just been invited by the Poynter Institute to spend a week as a guest faculty instructor in a skills seminar for news managers. The institute highlights best practices in the industry, so I was truly honored to speak about our newsroom's culture and how we produced award-winning journalism. I spent the rest of the week immersed in all the other sessions on management and leadership. I loved every minute of it.

Until we got to the session about coaching.

Teaching coaching skills to managers is a big deal at Poynter. That's because the media world is full of editors who fix writing but don't coach writers. It's common for them to make changes in stories rather than teach writers how to improve. Poynter faculty published a breakthrough book on the art of coaching writers, and the whole coach-don't-fix concept became part of the institute's DNA.

So there, in the session on coaching, instructors talked about the bad habits of fixers and their missed opportunities to raise quality. And they singled out one of the worst practices of inveterate fixers: They hijack people's work. They know what they want, so they just roll up their sleeves and *start rewriting reporters' stories for them.*

I wanted to slink out of the classroom. **They were describing me.**

I had been doing exactly that as a supervisor. Reporters gave me their stories to review and I'd rewrite whatever I thought needed strengthening. It was fast. It was efficient. But it did nothing for the employees whose stories I recrafted with my bare hands.

Now embarrassed—no, make that *ashamed*—I listened closely to everything in that session. Especially the part about how frustrating fixing can be to good employees who take pride in their work and would much prefer to get a little coaching from an editor and then polish their own work themselves.

I made a promise to myself: When I returned to my newsroom I would *sit on my hands.* No more leaping to the keyboard to make changes or corrections. I would learn to be a coach.

I kept that promise and reaped the benefits: higher quality, because I learned to *teach* rather than *do*—and happier employees, because I learned to keep my paws off their work and let them keep pride of authorship.

When you coach to improve people's skills, you do a lot of the same things as when you coach them about decisions: questioning, listening, and looking for options. You develop a vocabulary that specifically describes why something works or doesn't work well.

At the very beginning, coaching might take more time than making a quick fix to someone's work. Then that time investment pays dividends. The employee builds skills and you're not fixing the same things over and over.

Micromanaging and fixing isn't confined to only the industry where I worked. It happens in all professions, including yours. The world is awash in fixers. If you're among them, here are some persuasive reasons for you to start sitting on *your* hands, too:

THREE SINS OF FIXERS

• **Your more capable employees are frustrated.** You take their good work and add your signature touches to it. Is it better? Probably. But now it's not really theirs anymore—and you've undercut their important motivators: competence, progress, and autonomy. And don't assume everything's cool because they've never complained. It's not that easy to criticize the boss.

- **Your less capable employees are protected.** They don't have to grow because you're always there to fill their gaps. Their mediocre work actually looks pretty nice after you've tidied it up. You've trained them to rely on you to rescue them, and now they assume it's your responsibility.

- **You get worn down.** It's tiring to be a fixer. You spend way too much time putting out brushfires in the daily workflow and not enough on strategy, long-range planning, innovation—or even thinking. And you just can't figure out why some staffers still need help for the same issues, in spite of all your hard work.

That last point is very important. Being a fixer can lead to burnout. I want you to take better care of yourself. So I did just a little bit of editing to hammer home my message. I fixed the Fixer's Creed.

~~The Fixer's Creed:~~
~~Bring me your problems and I will give you solutions.~~
~~Show me your work and I will improve it, even if it~~
~~means doing it for you. It's my duty as a boss.~~

The Coach's Creed:
Bring me your problems and I will help you discover your own solutions. Show me your work and I will improve it by coaching, but I won't do it for you. It's my duty as a boss.

I think that's a change for the better. What do you think, coach?

All About the Workplace

How Great Bosses Build Great Places to Work

CHAPTER 12

Change Is the New Normal: Lead the Way

It's time for us to shift our focus. We began this leadership journey with an emphasis on *you*, then moved on to your *employees*. Now it's time to think bigger—about the *workplace*. Great bosses build environments where people can do good work—together.

It's about standards and systems and that word, "culture," which some people find hard to define, but boy, they know it when they have a good one—and hate it when they don't.

So as we look at the bigger picture, let's start with a reality check: Change has become the new normal in the world of work. Change is a constant, driven by two major forces: the economy and technology. If you want to build, maintain, and improve your workplace, you have to become adept at not just managing, but *leading* change.

Let's survey your situation. Think back over the last two years as you scan the list below. In which areas have significant changes taken place in your organization? Take a look at this list and check off every item that applies to you:

CHECK YOURSELF: WHAT'S CHANGED IN MY WORKPLACE LATELY?

- Top leadership
- My supervisor
- Size of our workforce
- Business strategy
- Business partners
- Tools and technology
- Our products/services
- Budgets
- Work rules/regulations
- Workflow
- Workload
- Workspace
- Work teams
- Employee compensation/benefits
- Employee duties/responsibilities
- My duties/responsibilities

My educated guess is that you gave your pen a workout in that exercise. Many of the managers I work with these days can check off every single item! And when they check the one labeled "size of our workforce," it isn't because they've added a whole lot of employees. That hasn't been the trend in a down economy.

Change takes place in the best of times, but today there's pressure to do more with less. As a boss, you must find savings where you can, keep quality high and your employees willing to keep fighting the good fight. It's not the impossible dream. Good bosses are making it happen. Just ask their employees—like this one, whose feedback is both positive and colorful:

> *She deals well with the screams and lamenting that come from those who work for her when change happens and new pressures develop . . . Most of the people who work for her are old-timers, so the cement around our ankles has hardened long ago. But as change happens, her grace and encouragement help us to accept change and embrace it.*

That quote made me smile. You may recall that in our chapter on communication, I discouraged bosses from using the term *"embrace* change" because it might sound too much like flowery management-speak. And yet here's a self-described "old-timer" using exactly that line to describe his state of mind—all because of his boss.

That's why I don't want you in a defensive crouch about change. I want you leading the charge, with this clear understanding:

Great bosses never assume the status quo is good enough.

You will do a great disservice to your organization, your people, and yourself if you believe that the best thing bosses do is guarantee stability and consistency. If that's the promise you make to your staff, the real world will make a liar of you. Instead, promise them that innovation and reinvention are realities you'll face together. Changing times demand leaders who can look people in the eyes and say:

- What we're doing is necessary and important.
- We can't waste time.
- *You* can do this; if things get tough, I'm here to help.
- We'll make mistakes as we move forward and we'll learn from them.
- Change doesn't mean we abandon our core values.

Say it. Then prove it.

LIGHTING A FIRE UNDER CHANGE

In my role as a leadership and management instructor, I have ingested more literature on the subject of change management than a normal person should endure. But I did it for a reason—to identify the best ideas and trends.

In addition to eyestrain, I took away this fundamental insight: Change involves two key challenges for people—learning and letting go.

Look back at your checklist. Each and every one of those changes underscores my point. People are faced with the challenge of learning new strategies, technology, tools, systems, workflow, and procedures—while letting go of past practices, assumptions, and even relationships.

They need your help.

Fortunately, if you've been working on all the skills we've discussed up to now, you're better prepared than ever to help people thrive during change. Notice that I said *thrive*—not survive. I have high expectations for you as their leader. Remember, change initiatives often fail, but not because they were bad ideas. They were good ideas, poorly executed. And since you're on the front lines of making things happen, I don't want you to fail.

Here are five things that make all the difference during change. They come up over and over as key factors in research about successful change. I call them **accelerators**, because if you handle them right, you can speed the process.

Five Change Accelerators

1. Education
2. Emotion
3. Motivation
4. Collaboration
5. Communication

Let's dig into them.

Managing the Five Change Accelerators

1. Education: Getting Smarter, Faster

Change requires us to learn new ways of doing things. We like to think of education as a wonderful gift. Learning makes us smarter, happier, and more valuable, right? But there's a huge roadblock that we ignore in our happy talk about learning.

Organizational psychologist Edgar Schein of MIT teaches something so simple but so profound that I repeat it to every class I teach on change: **Learning something new makes us temporarily incompetent.**

What an eye-opening truth. "Temporary incompetence" is the reason people so often resist the new. If you've ever dragged your feet rather than learn a new computer program, or never acted on your wish to learn another language, you know exactly what Schein's talking about. You hate *feeling* stupid and actually *being* stupid, even if only for a little while. You hate it even more when your incompetence is on display in the workplace for coworkers and bosses to see.

Schein refers to this as "learning anxiety"—people's fear of losing face and losing status in their organization, or even being punished for failing to achieve.

But here's the insight for managers: People rarely express their fears by saying, "I have learning anxiety about losing my status." Instead they say things to you like:

- "This is going to cause lots of problems."
- "Whose idea was this? It's not realistic."
- "This isn't the job I signed up for!"

Or they engage in passive resistance. They find all sorts of reasons to keep doing what they know, rather than facing the pain of learning what they don't. ("Aw, gee. So sorry I missed that training session, but you wanted me to finish this other project, remember?")

Now that you know what's really behind that resistance, you know how to respond.

- Don't engage in long debates with people about potential problems or whose idea this was.
- Don't assume all resisters are malcontents or slackers and pummel them with negative feedback.

You're wasting time and energy. Just calmly, firmly let people know you're moving forward and you want them with you. Talk about what they'll soon be doing better and why it matters. Tell them you have confidence in them and they'll be up to speed in no time. Tell them they're not in this alone. You've got their backs.

In other words, reduce their learning anxiety. How do you deliver on your promises? Give your people first-class training.

They deserve it—and frankly, they don't always get it. Trust me, I train people for a living. Here's the secret to quality training: Just as you can't treat everyone the same, don't assume that all adults learn the same. And by all means, don't assume they learn the same way you do.

When I'm teaching change accelerators in my workshops, I demonstrate this by asking the class this question:

"Who's purchased a new cell phone in the past year or so?"

Lots of hands go up. Then I ask people to tell me how they learned to use it. Here are the inevitable responses:

- "I read the manual."
- "I skip manuals. I like to learn by just playing with it."
- "I gave it to my kid to program for me."

- "I asked a friend who has one to walk me through the features. I like being able to ask someone questions as I learn."
- "I still haven't figured out all the features. I only use some of them."

It's a great reminder to custom-tailor your training whenever you can. Don't assume that one size fits all when it comes to learning, or that everyone learns everything in one session.

Experts in adult learning say we grown-ups don't take well to someone saying, "Memorize this, it will come in handy someday." We value learning that's practical, connects directly to our real world, and builds on things we already know. We want a say in how we're taught.

Use your coaching skills to ask people good questions about how they learn best. That will reduce their anxiety about jumping into the training pool and expedite their learning when they do.

Here's another tip about adult learners: You will waste your training efforts if there's a big lag time between when you offer training and when people actually *use* the new technology, tools, or systems. The new knowledge won't move from their short-term to their long-term memory unless they *act* on it.

One trainer at a newspaper told me he taught dozens of reporters how to use video cameras, as part of an effort to add multimedia reports to the paper's website. Reporters dutifully took the training, but afterward, many of their editors didn't ask them to shoot video while on assignment. As time passed and the reporters didn't practice, you can guess what happened. When it came time for them to use the cameras, they needed *retraining* to do it.

The lesson: Training has to be part of a master plan that involves the whole organization. Three steps are necessary:

Step 1: Provide top-notch training for new skills.
Step 2: Put the new knowledge to immediate use.
Step 3: Provide ongoing feedback to employees as they try new things.

To that last point, feedback is a two-way street. Just as you let people know how well they're doing, don't forget to ask *them* for feedback, too. You'll find out what they need from you now, and how training might improve in the future.

There's another way to assess training. **Become a student yourself.** I'm not saying you must attend every training session or learn every skill required of your employees. Be strategic about it. Pick something that's important to your team. Learn alongside people as a show of solidarity—and an opportunity to evaluate how well your organization accelerates change with quality education.

2. Emotion: You Can Hurry Love

Some managers believe that emotion has no place in the workplace, where reason should rule. They're all business, thank you. They think that if they make a rational case to employees and state unequivocally that things must be different, then change will follow.

But Harvard business professor John Kotter, one of the preeminent experts on organizational change, has another view. He believes successful change is built on understanding and managing **emotions**. He chose the title of his book *The Heart of Change* as a way to underscore his message. According to Kotter, we can dump all the data we want on people about the business case for change, but they don't respond to cold statistics. They respond to something they personally experience that triggers their emotions. His formula is:

People don't: "Analyze-Think-Change"
What they really do is: "See-Feel-Change"

See-Feel-Change was the theory behind the cell phone exercise I just told you about. My goal was to *change the managers' approach to training*. Under the Analyze-Think-Change model, I would have shown the managers a Power-Point about the "Principles of Andragogy" (adult learning), complete with bullet points about "task-orientation," "customization," and "experiential learning." I'm sure most would have taken notes—but would they even remember later? And if they remembered, would it have made enough of an impression that it moved them to change?

Compare that to the See-Feel-Change approach, with their personal experiences as the focus. When I asked the cell phone questions, they laughed while sharing their answers and—wow, would you look at that?—They **discovered** the diverse learning styles *among people just like them*.

I set them up to experience the emotion of **surprise**, **amusement**, and even a little **embarrassment** about what they didn't know and how it could impede their work in managing change. Now add to that my real world story about the video training that went to waste—teeing up a little **fear**: "Yikes, I better not let something like that happen to my team!"—and you can see where emotion can be far more persuasive than cold statistics.

So, as Kotter teaches, don't just *tell* people things, *show* them truths that touch their emotions and move them to change their behaviors. Dramatic, concrete, real-life examples are your best friend.

There's another way to leverage the power of emotion in managing change: Help people score some "quick wins."

Quick wins are small successes at the beginning of an initiative that give people a jolt of confidence. They can also provoke a bandwagon effect among the troops. Employees who've been holding back will *see* a real-life example of a victory, *feel* confidence or even competitiveness, and *change* by deciding to get with the program.

So with apologies to singer Diana Ross for changing the title to one of her classic hits, you *can* hurry love.

I wish I could end our lesson on emotion there, but we haven't dealt with the full scope of emotions during change. There are times you have to deal with **heartache**. It can be among the hardest things you do as a manager.

Employees experience anger, grief, and guilt when change involves downsizing. People they care about are gone. Projects they built or believe in have been canceled. They've lost money or benefits or status in the workplace during traumatic change—and you've been a part of making that happen, directly or indirectly, because you are part of the management team.

This is when your emotional intelligence skills must be

at their very best. I like the advice offered in the book *Healing the Wounds: Overcoming the Trauma of Layoffs and Revitalizing Downsized Organizations*. Author David Noer says managers should lead from the heart and follow with the head. Don't respond to emotion with business jargon. Respond with empathy. Listen. Acknowledge employees' legitimate feelings.

People will always remember—for better or worse—how managers respond after downsizing. If it happens on your watch, would you want them saying something like this:

"They acted like we should just move on and not discuss it. They were all business—as if they didn't care about anything but the bottom line."

Or could your actions produce this kind of response:

"They didn't ignore how much this means to us. They let us vent. You could see it wasn't easy. They listened and if we had questions, they did their best to answer."

Your empathy will help people through their initial strong negative emotions. At the very least, you won't be making a bad situation worse. At best, you will be accelerating the healing that has to take place in order to keep people from being paralyzed by anger or fear.

Here's feedback that shows how one boss did just that:

With good grim humor, she has helped lead us through severe downsizing. She has done this by reminding us what our core mission is, and if we focus on that we'll be all right.

And she has led by example, by just getting down to work and not whining, and proving we can do it.

Remember the power of emotion during change—in the worst times and in the everyday ebb and flow of taking risks and trying new things. And don't forget that you're contagious, boss. Your openness and optimism set the tone for your team.

3. Motivation: Let Them Help Drive

I always include motivation in my list of change accelerators, and since you've studied motivation in chapter 8, you already understand why. In fact, I bet you already connected the dots when I wrote, "Learning something new makes us temporarily incompetent." You remembered that **competence** and **growth** are intrinsic motivators. That people want to do more of what they're good at—and what makes them feel they're growing. You recognized that if you don't do everything possible to help them overcome learning anxiety, you are demotivating people and slowing down the very change you're driving for.

And if you're smart, you'll share the driver's seat with them.

As a manager who knows about motivation, you know the power of **autonomy**, which gives employees choice and voice. People fall in love with their own ideas and solutions. So when you're looking to change systems or brainstorm innovation, get your team involved on the front end. Enlist their ideas. Get them invested.

Sometimes a project demands secrecy for competitive or legal reasons. But if that's not the case, think twice before springing a *fully formed* change initiative on people. When you do that, they'll direct their intellectual energies toward finding and dissecting its weak points, rather than advancing the plan because they helped develop it.

Getting people involved on the front end is a balancing act. Provide enough of a vision of where you want to end up before you turn over the keys. Share a vivid picture of the destination and invite them to help you fill in the map and share the driving.

Then, of course, there's the intrinsic motivator of **purpose**. I've noted that change involves learning and *letting go*. In the uncertainty or ambiguity of trying new things and taking risks, people may feel they are letting go of things that have meaning to them. In their minds and hearts, "the way we've always done things" may epitomize quality. It's up to you to underscore the value and purpose of the new.

Take a look at how employees respond when a boss does this well:

He is good at rallying the troops, making you feel like you are part of something important. When we launched our team's new product, we were kind of out there on our own. He helped instill the confidence we needed to get going and do great work. He's also a natural teacher, able to explain things in a way that's easy to understand and easy to implement, without the B.S., which we all appreciate.

Clear message to managers: Speed up change by turning emerging competence to solid confidence. Go heavy on the meaningfulness, light on the B.S. And let them help you drive.

4. Collaboration: Tear Down Your Silo

Today's flatter organizations depend on collaboration: less turf protection, more sharing. That's an important change. But there's often a roadblock to that change—one that may surprise you. *Team-building* by bosses can work too well—and impede collaboration across the organization.

Here's a typical team-building situation: The boss works hard to build esprit de corps in the work group or department. The employees now share an identity ("We're the marketers who get things done," or "We're the tech wizards"). The team members are on the same page about goals, quality, budgets, and resources. So what's the downside? Proud and perfectly functioning *teams* turn into *silos*.

Silos are insular groups that may do fine work, but don't play well with others. Silos take care of their own...period. They can hold back change, impede innovation, and cause unnecessary expense.

Here's a quick look at the differences:

CHARACTERISTICS OF TEAMS AND SILOS	
Teams	**Silos**
Common identity	Common identity
Share info	Guard info
See big picture of organization	See picture of own goals
Network across groups	Avoid outreach
"Us and Them"	"Us versus Them"
Boss's style: Collaborative	Boss's style: Controlling

As you look at that chart, you can see the downside of silos. You can also see that the boss plays a key role in the problem.

I don't want this to sound like an indictment of the bosses. In fact, I think it is a classic Evil Twin situation. The managers never saw their style as "controlling." In their minds, they were "protecting." Their intention was to keep their team on track and not get taken advantage of by other departments. But while tending to the well-being and success of their people, managers can become gatekeepers who tightly control access to the group and its talent.

It's time to turn them loose. Managers in today's organizations need to take a global approach to the whole business, not just their team's piece of it. To succeed today, you must network across the organization like never before.

There's a term that describes this so well, one that comes up over and over in the book *Hot Spots: Why Some Teams, Workplaces, and Organizations Buzz with Energy—and Others Don't*. In it, Lynda Gratton of the London Business School writes about "boundary spanners." She describes them as people who naturally network, exchange information, and solve problems. As she studies innovation in companies and finds pockets of exceptional performance, boundary spanners are key to the success. They are motivated by a challenge or opportunity and they contribute their talent with a genuine spirit of cooperation.

Some people may be born to span boundaries, but anyone can achieve that distinction. It's a matter of choice and commitment. As a boss, you have the power to accelerate that. First, **be a role model**. Stop protecting/controlling and start collaborating. Set the tone for your team. Then reward and reinforce employees for being your boundary spanners. Soon it will be second nature to your whole team—which, by the way, bears no resemblance to a silo.

5. Communication

Here's the key to communication in times of change:

- You need to repeat yourself a lot.
- You need to repeat yourself a lot.

There are several reasons for this:

1. **What's clear to you isn't clear to everyone else.** You've had this change on your mind longer than your staff has. You've been involved in management-level conversations about the need for it and the next steps. You've processed both the information and the emotion. You've moved on to the acceptance and action phase. But your staff is just hearing things for the first time. It's going to take them a while to process the news, too. That usually takes more than one conversation. They have more questions. More concerns. More need for information from you.

2. **Every employee has questions. They ask at different times.** You may have shared your message in a meeting, but people want to ask, "What does this mean to me?" in one-on-one sessions later. Never assume a group meeting is sufficient. Don't even wait for people to come to you. If you want to accelerate change, work the room. Invite questions. Then do it again.

3. **If you don't talk, others will—and they might be wrong.** Rumors run rampant during change. If you're not

available to repeat the facts, the bad information out there can take on a life of its own—and slow down your change. In times of major change, smart management teams plan for rumor control and response. When thinking about change, they have an FAQ mindset from the start. What might people ask—including the toughest questions? If we don't have answers, our silence can send the wrong messages.

Until now, you may have assumed that change is inevitably a slow process. Think again. In their book *Hard Facts, Dangerous Half-Truths, and Total Nonsense: Profiting from Evidence-Based Management*, Stanford business professors Jeffrey Pfeffer and Robert Sutton say change can happen quickly when there's dissatisfaction with the status quo and leaders confidently outline a clear new direction. Once again, communication is key. Their advice:

Relentlessly communicate what the change is, why it is necessary, and what people ought to be doing right now, with as much clarity as possible. If you aren't saying, writing and modeling the same message over and over again, it probably isn't going to stick.

Relentlessly communicate. Lead with the heart and then the head. Build competence, confidence, and collaboration. Do all that and you'll not only expedite change; your employees will applaud you. Like this:

She's got a knack—we can call it a gift, maybe—for making me feel better about a hill we need to climb, or climb again in a different way. It's never a Knute Rockne pregame speech, but many times she's helped me see: (1) Why this hill is an objective; (2) That she is fully aware of the difficulty; (3) That I'm not the only climber. She's probably the best boss I ever had.

NOTE THE NEW NORMAL: CELEBRATING CHANGE

I'm confident that your new change management skills are going to serve you well. You'll guide your team through transitions and innovation in your workplace—and when it works out well, people will be proud of the outcomes.

I think it's important for managers to tell stories that remind people how far they've come, to celebrate the work people did to learn and grow, and to reinforce the positive values that underpin the updated ways of doing things.

It will help smooth the way for the next change, and the next.

Let's end this chapter with a self-assessment. I've used variations of this "Change Checkup" with teams of managers in organizations. After I teach about the five change accelerators, the managers answer the checkup questions and discuss their responses. The goal is to generate a candid self-assessment, action steps—and change.

CHANGE CHECKUP
CHECK YOURSELF: ARE WE
ACCELERATING CHANGE?

EDUCATION

1. How strong is our commitment to training? What do we do well?

2. Do managers attend or observe employee training, especially when the training is related to an important change?

3. Do we strategically coordinate training with "doing," giving employees opportunities to use the skills, not lose them over time?

EMOTION

1. Are managers in this organization encouraged to plan for and respond to the emotions of employees during change?

2. How well do we handle emotion? What could we do better?

3. Do managers help employees achieve "quick wins" during change, to build momentum?

MOTIVATION

1. How well do our managers understand and encourage motivation—especially intrinsic motivation?

2. Do we involve employees, whenever possible, in designing and carrying out change initiatives?

3. Do we provide sufficient feedback during change, so people don't lose confidence in their competence?

COLLABORATION

1. Do we have any silos in our organization? If so, what will it take to transform them back into collaborative teams?

2. Who are the "boundary spanners" in our organization—both managers and staff?

3. What could we do to encourage better networking and collaboration?

COMMUNICATION

1. Do we plan a communication strategy when introducing change?

2. How well do we handle rumors?

3. When we've been at our best as communicators, what was it that we did differently or better?

Based on our answers to these questions, what ACTION STEPS will we take?

Our next stop: a close look at what's working well—and what could work better—in your workplace.

CHAPTER 13

What's It Really Like to Work Here, Boss?

I hired a lot of people in my many years as a manager. When a promising job candidate was in my office for an interview, my side of the conversation usually included these three statements:

1. "We think you could make us better."
2. "My management philosophy is simple: Life's too short to work with jerks."
3. And this, which I never thought of as a risky offer: "I've told you a lot of good things about this place, but don't take my word for it. Go out there and spend time talking with everyone on staff. Ask whatever you want. Find out what it's *really* like to work here."

My staff helped me hire some great people.

That's what I want for you: to be able to sing the praises of your people, your product, your systems, and your standards—and know that your staff, speaking freely, would say, "Amen." I want you to build the kind of place where people enjoy coming to work.

Obviously, you should strive to make certain your employees are paid fairly and their work environment is safe and comfortable. I won't presume to tell you precisely what those wages should be or what colors to paint your walls.

Instead, I want to talk with you about issues that come up repeatedly when people describe good **workplace cultures**. You won't be surprised to discover the signs all point right back to *you, the leader*, and the choices you make each day. You'll soon discover that the skills you've been building, chapter by chapter in this book, now start coming together with a big payoff. This is where "work happy" becomes a reality.

I'm going to guide you through **five indicators of a positive, healthy culture**—with tips for each. Here's a quick preview:

1. Employees know it's not a democracy, but their voices matter.
2. The boss plays favorites—and everyone's a potential favorite. (Really!)
3. Employees work well together because the boss breaks down barriers.
4. People actually get things done in meetings!
5. Mistakes create a climate of learning, not fear.

Here's a look at each:

Work Happy: Five Symptoms of a Healthy Culture

Healthy Culture Symptom #1: Employees know it's not a democracy, but their voices matter.

The world of work, by its very nature, isn't "government by the people." Employees rarely get to choose their CEOs, set their own rules, or determine their own salaries. It's not a democracy, and though they might prefer it were otherwise, they accept it. But what they don't want is a dictatorship—also known as a top-down management. In top-down cultures, bosses don't just manage, they *rule*.

When there's a decision to be made in a top-down culture, it's automatically assumed that bosses know best. Employees should comply, period. What drives this? Actually, some very old-school thinking that you should know about.

Top-down cultures are rooted in what legendary psychologist/business professor Douglas McGregor called "Theory X." Theory X says human beings dislike work and avoid it. They don't want responsibility, and therefore they must be tightly supervised and directed, lest they goof off. But in his breakthrough management book *The Human Side of Enterprise*, published way back in 1960, McGregor challenged that notion.

He introduced "Theory Y," which says that work is a natural part of life, people don't inherently dislike it, and they do better when they're encouraged and involved in decisions about their work and workplace. That theory guides a good deal of management teaching today. But it still hasn't killed top-down cultures. They exist wherever managers hold tightly to power and don't share it.

There's an easy test of how tight the grip is: Look at daily decision-making. Check out who has a voice and who doesn't.

Back in chapter 6, when we talked about managing your time, we stressed the importance of knowing when to delegate and when to do things yourself. The focus was mainly on keeping you from taking on too much responsibility and burning yourself out. In chapter 11, I warned you about the dangers of too much fixing and not enough coaching. But now I want to underscore the *workplace benefit* that comes when you, the boss, don't hoard the power: When you share responsibility and authority, you build a better, stronger culture.

Don't think your only options are to do things yourself or to delegate. When it comes to making judgment calls, you have an array of choices. Here's a look at the spectrum:

POWER-SHARING OPTIONS IN DECISION-MAKING

- **Command Decision:** I decide.

- **Consultative Decision:** I ask for input; then I decide.

- **Delegated Decision:** I decide that someone else should decide.

- **Democratic Decision:** I put it to a team vote; majority rules.

- **Consensus Decision:** I help my group come to a decision everyone can live with.

In top-down cultures, bosses stay in the "command" zone and occasionally dabble in "consultative." Unfortunately, it's often "faux-consultative." Their employees describe it this way: "They come in with their minds made up, go through the motions of asking our opinions, and then do what they want anyway."

It doesn't have to be that way. In shared-power cultures, managers use the full range of options. The staff understands that it's a business, not a democracy, and that their bosses make executive decisions for good reasons. They also know their bosses try to include employee ideas and voices whenever possible—not just to be nice or to be liked, but because it's good for business. Psychologist Daniel Levi, in his book *Group Dynamics for Teams*, says:

> In general, decision-making techniques that include group discussion and participation lead to higher quality decisions; this is especially true if the problems are complex or unstructured, or if leaders do not have enough information to make good decisions.

So tap the brains of your team members. Don't worry, I'm not telling you to call a meeting and take a vote for every decision. Think about three key factors when deciding how to decide:

- **Quality:** What information is needed to make the best decision? Do I have enough? Whose input would make it better?
- **Speed:** How much time do we have?
- **Acceptance:** How will the decision style affect the employees' acceptance and implementation of the decision?

That last point—acceptance—is very important. People are more likely to support decisions into which they've had input. Buy-in accelerates implementation.

Compare that to top-down cultures where bosses don't care about acceptance and simply demand **compliance**. They may get it, but the compliance is often grudging, slow, and spotty, because employees are demotivated.

If you want to be a great boss, build a reputation for sharing power and decision-making with people at all levels of your organization. When you share the decision-making power, be clear with people about which style you're invoking and why. Here are some illustrations for each variety:

Command Decision: I decide.

As I emphasized in chapter 6, your staff understands—and even appreciates—when you invoke executive decision-making for issues that are urgent, critical, or risky. Your expertise and rank in the organization make you the ideal decision-maker. A command decision sounds like this:

> "This would be a direct violation of the contract we just negotiated. Moreover, it's fundamentally unfair to staff. This is an easy call. We won't do this."

Tip: Many command decisions involve the need for confidentiality—from business negotiations to firings. I've learned over my years of management that if you build trust with employees, they accept it when you look them in the eye and say, "This was my decision. I'm not able to go into detail beyond that. I trust that you understand." Your credibility pays off when you clearly must go it alone, and you make it clear to staff that they won't have input.

Consultative Decision: I ask for input; then I decide.

This style is an excellent choice when you want to improve the quality of the decision and the acceptance level among staff. You're mining for ideas and opinions. It takes a little more time than command, but it doesn't always have to. You don't have to turn every consultation into a meeting. Sometimes you just touch base with people quickly by phone or email.

The key is to be clear with people that you are interested in their ideas and views, but not taking a vote:

> "Could I pick your brain about your experience working with this supplier? I'm interested in input, but just know that because of big dollars and the complexity of this project, the final call will be mine."

Tip: After making your decision, try to **close the loop** with the people you consulted, especially if you didn't go in the direction they suggested. A few quick words from you will keep them from feeling rejected or dismissed, and keep you from getting a reputation for only *pretending* to be inclusive.

Delegated Decision: I decide that someone else should decide.

Deciding who decides is a true management skill. You're analyzing both the nature of the decision and the expertise of the person to whom you delegate. If things go wrong, you can't just delegate blame; the mess still happened on your watch. I say this not to scare you away from delegating, but to encourage you to do *more* of it, wisely. If you start with the idea that you want to share power, then you're constantly scoping out opportunities to delegate, and at the same time working with your staff so their skills are up to the assignment.

Delegation sounds like this:

> "You know the clients and the project history better than I do. I'll trust your decision on whether to discount our fee within the range we discussed. Let me know what you decide so I can budget accordingly."

Tip: It's important to let the person know if you wish to be informed about the decision, and why. It keeps you from appearing to be setting up an opportunity to second-guess or overrule.

Democratic Decision: I put it to a team vote; majority rules.

The good part about democratic decisions is that everyone gets a vote. The bad part is that whenever the vote isn't unanimous, some people lose—and losing isn't fun. That's why democratic decisions often work best when the stakes *aren't high*. That way, losers won't be bruised and won't passively or actively obstruct the decision's implementation. Here's an example:

> "We have two excellent alternatives for the logo design. Either one would be terrific. Let's just put it to a vote and go with what the majority likes best."

Tip: Should you take part in a democratic vote? Maybe. Let's say you are discussing moving the staff picnic from July to August, as some staffers have suggested. If you say, "Let's go around the table and each of us gets a vote," two things happen: You put yourself on an equal footing with everyone else on the team—a nice gesture. You also put people in the position of voting against the boss. If you have a reputation for sharing power and being a good sport, there's no problem. But if people don't know you well, you could intimidate without even knowing it. Use your good judgment to decide whether to play or abstain. Abstaining also sends a positive message: "I trust your collective wisdom, team."

Consensus Decision: I help my group come to a decision everyone can live with.

Consensus decision-making is often the most time-consuming, because there's a good amount of talking and listening, often with a facilitator who may or may not be the boss. It's usually done when you want people to be really invested in a decision, but they have different perspectives that need to be reconciled.

For example, let's say you've finally gotten funding to hire your first summer intern. You want it to go well, so you can turn it into an ongoing program. You invite your team to help you select from several good candidates. Your team members have different viewpoints. Some believe students from local schools should get preference. Others say the school shouldn't be a deciding factor, only the student's skills. Instead of putting it to a vote, you ask the group to talk about what really matters most, the goals they all share for this experiment to turn into a long-term success. You encourage them to come up with a decision that everyone can find value in, even if it isn't everyone's first choice.

If you've built a positive workplace culture, even consensus decision-making can happen efficiently because people trust and support each other. They know they get a voice often enough that they don't have to *fight* for the opportunity to have a say in "how we do things around here."

Healthy Culture Symptom #2: The boss plays favorites—and everyone's a potential favorite. (Really!)

I may throw you a curve with this one, but I tell managers that they can and should "play favorites." But they have to take ownership of what that term means. By playing favorites, I mean you are identifying **exceptional employees** and giving them important assignments, learning opportunities, coveted work shifts, and participation in key projects and decisions.

Stay with me on this. I know the term "playing favorites" has the stench of unfairness all over it, no doubt because of all the bosses who favored certain employees over others for reasons that are clearly wrong.

Here are some of the *worst* reasons bosses could anoint a staffer as a "favorite":

- She's an **employee I hired**, not one I inherited.
- He **reminds me of me**; we share the same gender, ethnicity, or generation.
- We share the same **outside interests**—perhaps sports, music, or church work.
- We share the same **vices**; our stolen moments in smoke breaks bond us.

- She's a **favorite of my supervisor**, who is blind to her flaws; I haven't figured out how to right that wrong.
- He's a **world-class suck-up** and his flattery is irresistible.
- We came up together in the organization; you have to look out for your **old friends**.

Bosses who make choices like that are the reason "playing favorites" has such a bad name—and why I want to change it. I want you to be able to say, with absolute clarity, how a person becomes a "favorite" employee in your workplace, and how you select people for promotions, privileges, or opportunities. Remember, you don't treat everyone the same. You know them well, play to their strengths, do your best to help them grow, and make your standards clear.

Give everyone a fair shot, then play favorites for all the right reasons. The meaning changes when you select the *best* candidates for "favorite" status. Consider these:

- She's a consistently **outstanding performer who's always willing to help** others.
- He's a talented staff member who demonstrates commitment to growth; he's the **role model for learning**.
- She's **an early adopter and a pacesetter** as we're trying to get people to do things differently in times of change.
- He's an **innovative problem-solver** who looks out for the team's best interests.
- She's **one of those boundary spanners**, someone who builds bonds across silos in the organization and looks for opportunities to improve the work.

- He's **"buried treasure,"** a high-quality staff member who, for some reason, was overlooked by previous managers and deserves an opportunity to finally shine.
- She's a **"comeback kid,"** who responded to feedback and coaching, made a remarkable and consistent improvement, and has earned respect for the effort.

Now, here's the tricky part:

Sometimes, an employee can fit into both categories. That high performer may also be the same gender or ethnicity as you, the boss. That boundary spanner may have indeed come up with you in the organization. That "buried treasure" guy may attend your church.

Unless you make it absolutely clear to the staff why you give certain people coveted assignments, roles, shifts, or training, I guarantee that the rest of the staff will attribute it to the WORST reasons.

Your respect and reputation will be diminished among staff. Your "favored" employees may be criticized or ostracized by their peers, which is unfair to them, especially because you don't install "favorites for life"—they must continuously earn that distinction.

That's the most important point about a culture of playing favorites for all the right reasons. It's not a closed clubhouse. It's a meritocracy. As the leader, you provide the high-quality feedback you studied in chapters 9 and 10, and you reward people for being living, breathing examples of what you value in your workplace culture.

Those "favorites" are really your standard bearers. Everyone knows why—and how they, too, can qualify.

Healthy Culture Symptom #3: Employees work well together because the boss breaks down barriers.

Who doesn't want to work in a culture where people happily share information and resources, understand and appreciate each other's responsibilities, and help each other succeed?

We may want it. But we don't always get it.

Here's what I've discovered: Even if you follow my mantra of "life's too short to work with jerks" and hire people who are inclined to play well with others, and even if you reward people for being boundary spanners, you still may not achieve the collaborative results you want. That's because there are four barriers that often get in the way of the best-intentioned employees. They are barriers that only *you* can demolish, boss. I believe **the four big barriers to collaboration are**:

1. **Distance**
2. **Dominance**
3. **Dissonance**
4. **Discomfort**

Let's break them down, so to speak.

1. The Distance Barrier

When employees work in varied places, from different rooms to different cities, or when they work in the same place but on different shifts, the absence of face-to-face contact can be a roadblock to collaboration. It inevitably sets the table for misunderstandings. People slip off each other's radar screens. They have less awareness, appreciation, and empathy regarding one another's workloads, successes, or challenges.

Your Role as Leader

Be vigilant about how easily people can lapse into misjudging and misunderstanding people with whom they don't have regular contact and high-quality communication.

Remind people that face-to-face interaction is best, followed by video chats, phone conversations, and email, in that order. Remind them that email, however speedy, carries with it all the dangers we discussed in chapter 5—**and those dangers are enhanced by distance**. If people are in disagreement and are distant from each other, advise them to step back from their keyboards.

Look at **the layout of your workspace** and assess whether, especially in changing times, it works as well as it should. Is it time to rearrange the furniture to decrease distance between people, or perhaps to create new spaces where people from different work groups can meet to plan or brainstorm? (Reminder: Modifying workspace affects employees both professionally and personally. It's a test of the change management skills you learned in chapter 12.)

When planning training or even social events, **think of yourself as a matchmaker**, casting diverse people together for the express purpose of building stronger working relationships—and spanning boundaries.

2. The Dominance Barrier

If leaders want the staff to work as partners, they can't turn a blind eye to the perceived or real hierarchies in the workplace. Organizational cultures often create their own caste systems among categories of work and workers, *while still maintaining that everyone should cooperate and collaborate.*

It could be white-collar workers, artists, tech experts, or PhDs, who, by all assumptions, are just "higher on the food chain around this place." And those assumptions may be a barrier to their playing well with others.

Similarly, flawed bosses who play favorites for the *worst* reasons may also let their pet employees lord it over others. Hence my insistence that in establishing the qualifications for *your* favorites, your definition of high performance should always include *collaboration*.

Your Role as Leader

Take an honest accounting of whether there is an unspoken, understood, but possibly unfair power structure among employees. Is it based on tenure, roles and responsibilities, relationships or expertise? Are there people who assume, or have been encouraged to assume, that others are expected to serve their interests, first and foremost? If that's the way you want it—that's your call as a boss. But then don't use the term "collaboration" to describe what is really "accommodation" by *some* staff members to the wishes and needs of others. Collaboration means mutual support and mutual sacrifice, as people work together toward a shared goal. Which one *really* describes what it's like to work around here?

3. The Dissonance Barrier

This barrier pops up when bosses pile so many duties on employees that in order to survive, they just hunker down and take care of their own needs. The employer's messages are contradictory: Get all these assignments done in the time frame and to the specifications I demand—but also dedicate your time and resources to helping others. That dissonance drives people bonkers—and into bunkers. Even if they want to help their colleagues, they back away out of self-preservation.

Your Role as Leader

Keep track of workloads. Consider whether you contribute to their stress and time challenges. Late notice, poor organization, unclear instructions or priorities—all make work more difficult and workers less likely to be able to reach out to engage with others. Understand what it takes to accomplish the tasks you give people and what else is going on in their world. If your people have the skill and will to collaborate and it's not happening the way you'd like, ask for candid feedback about what you can do to remove the dissonance barrier.

Even the highly regarded, highly collaborative leaders need reminders. Check out this feedback—a perfect example of a tactful nudge to a popular boss who supervises cross-team projects:

> *When we work on projects together with staff, she gives me room to do my job, and have fun doing my job, while providing support. Other than my direct manager, there's no one I would rather work with on something . . . Okay, I'm saying this only because I feel compelled to provide something other than lavish praise! On rare occasions, perhaps because she has been in the company for so long and IS so knowledgeable, she assumes she knows how something is working/ should work in an area. I would just encourage her to hear out the people doing the work daily, to hear what competing values they are weighing in deciding how to do what they do.*

Listening can help you resolve the dissonance.

4. The Discomfort Barrier

It can be difficult for employees to buddy up with someone they don't really know and whose skill set is foreign to them. It's so much easier for workers to stay in their comfort zones, where there's common vocabulary, tools, and knowledge. Left to their own devices, employees may shy away from working with those whose expertise makes them feel incompetent or whose work doesn't seem interesting. Why go through the hassle, just because the boss wants everyone to play nicely together on projects?

Your Role as Leader

You can't just focus on the product; you have to lead people. That means guiding them to a better understanding and appreciation of each other, their roles, and their responsibilities. It means finding ways to educate the whole workplace about the contributions of each team and its members. It means rewarding those who span boundaries, network well, and help others.

Let me offer a simple and powerful way to break the discomfort barrier. Try it yourself and then encourage your employees to do the same. Think about the people in your workplace who do jobs unlike your own, people you either work with now or might in the future. Once you've identified them, set about to find out:

"What makes a great day at work for you?"

It's a disarming question, one I've used when working with diverse teams. They may start out by joking that a great day is "when no one bugs me" or "when the vending machine isn't out of Snickers bars." Don't dismiss those responses, because they might provide a little human insight. But don't stop there. Here's the information that you really want to learn:

- What do their bosses expect of them? How do they measure success?
- What professional standards are really meaningful in their specialty area? (When they talk about the "all-time greats" in their field, what is it they do so darn well?)
- What personal goals have they set for themselves?
- What are they really proud of?
- Who in the organization "gets it"—that is, knows just how to work with them to get things done with maximum success and minimum hassle? What do they do differently from other people?

This isn't an interrogation, of course. It's a friendly conversation you may have in a break room over coffee or on the job over time. (It could also be a fun exercise at a staff workshop.)

Approach this with the spirit of those feedback glasses I told you about in chapter 9. Just as you look for feedback opportunities all around you, you are also on the alert for "great day" insights about work groups in your organization. It's the essence of the relationship management aspect of emotional intelligence we covered in chapter 4, and is a powerful force for breaking down collaboration barriers.

Healthy Culture Symptom #4: People actually get things done in meetings!

Mention the word "meeting" and people often roll their eyes—but different reasons drive that disdain for each of us. Too many meetings or too few. Too meandering or too scripted. Too dominated by certain people or beliefs. Too much talk, not enough results. Any of those complaints sound familiar to you? If so, you have the power to change things, and you should.

Meetings are a reflection of your workplace culture—its strengths and its weaknesses. It's a point echoed by management scholars Terrence Deal and Allan Kennedy in their book *Corporate Cultures: The Rites and Rituals of Corporate Life*:

> Forget the stated purpose of the meeting. Instead, keep track of what is actually discussed—and who talks, and to whom. Track how much time is spent on each subject. However surprising the result—and we guarantee you will be surprised—you'll discover that the culture spends its time on what it values most.

Are you dealing with what is supposed to matter most in your meetings? In positive cultures, meetings are focused on the right goal. The participants are frank but friendly, and everyone is heard.

To help you assess and improve the quality of your meetings, I have two gifts for you—a breakdown of meeting types and goals, and then a checklist to help you evaluate yours.

SIX GOOD REASONS TO CALL A MEETING

1. **To provide timely information.** These meetings involve announcements or status reports shared among colleagues.

2. **To give direction.** This is the huddle before the play; the review of roles, responsibilities, and goals.

3. **To make group decisions.** These confabs give people a voice in a pending matter.

4. **To produce a product.** The team is together to create something right there, or produce some part of it.

5. **To generate ideas and solutions.** The group is brainstorming or problem-solving.

6. **To observe rituals.** People gather to celebrate, share, bond, and make memories.

Even when meeting conveners *think* they know why the meeting is necessary, the gathering still may go astray. Here are the two main reasons:

- **Lack of focus.** Meeting types merge into each other, and not because they have to. The goal of the meeting isn't clear, so it becomes a runaway train—or a stalled one.

- **Lack of discipline.** With no clear rules of the road for behavior, meetings can become playgrounds or battlegrounds, meander off-task, and have no follow-up.

That's why it pays to step back and evaluate the quality and quantity of your meetings. Here's a checklist so you can give yours a going-over. Make a list of your meetings—especially those that you think could be improved, or even discontinued—and apply these questions.

CHECK YOURSELF: MANAGE YOUR MEETING!

1. On a scale of 1 to 10, with 10 being the "most"—how important is this meeting to our organization and its goals? _____

2. Does this meeting have an agenda and format to help people prepare and keep us on track? Should it? _____

3. Does the right person lead the meeting? Do we have other options? How might different leadership alter the meeting? _____

4. Do the right people attend this meeting? Is anyone missing? Are some people here out of habit rather than necessity? _____

5. Do the people at this meeting contribute meaningfully? If not, why—and what can we do to improve participation? _____

6. How well do we stay on track? What or who causes us to lose focus? What can we do to minimize distractions and drift? _____

(Continued)

> 7. Do we end each meeting with a clear understanding of next steps, roles, responsibilities, deadlines, and how we communicate between meetings?
> _____
>
> 8. If we stopped holding this meeting, what would happen? What harm might we cause or good might we do? What alternatives would we develop to accomplish the meeting's goals? _____

I'm not as cranky about meetings as the late, legendary management sage Peter Drucker, who said:

Meetings are by definition a concession to deficient organization. For one either meets or works.

But I hope by assessing your meetings carefully, you'll sort the necessary from the needless, improve every meeting you manage—and your people will say, "We get things done in ours!"

Healthy Culture Symptom #5: Mistakes create a climate of learning, not fear.

Q: What happens when bosses mishandle workplace mistakes?

A: You build a culture of fear, stupid. How could you not know that?

That's how it feels to work in an unhealthy culture, where the reaction to mistakes is a toxic mix of humiliation and vengeance. Now, let me state for the record: I believe people *should fear making mistakes*—not because they'll be pummeled and pilloried, but because they'll be letting others down: their customers, their coworkers, and themselves.

That's not a culture of fear; it's a culture of accountability—and learning.

The challenge, of course, is that you must do this while not being a "too-nice boss" who creates a culture of mediocrity. You are the steward of your organization's quality and reputation. Mistakes are, in fact, your enemy, so you can't afford to mishandle them.

Here are three common management personas in the face of mistakes:

The exploder: A boss who believes the ferocity of his or her response is justified in the defense of quality and assumes people are motivated by fear. The exploder prefers the role of prosecutor and avenger.

The excuser: A boss who treads lightly around mistakes, assuming they reflect his or her personal failures as much as anyone else's, and fears staff morale could crumble under criticism. The excuser prefers the role of defender.

The explorer: A boss who wants to know the why and how of a mistake, and works with the offender to determine exactly what went wrong so it will not happen again. The explorer prefers the role of investigator and tough-but-fair teacher.

I'm a fan of the third option. I think explorers produce more effective long-term solutions. Their analytical approach may identify gaps in training, communication, policies, systems, roles, responsibilities, and accountability. While **not letting offenders off the hook**, explorers also seek to eliminate current and future excuses for goof-ups.

Explorers aren't wimps—as evidenced by this feedback received by a manager whose staff described her as smart, direct, and decisive:

> *She's honestly one of the strongest women I've ever met. Once I made a mistake in an email to someone and she simply sat me down, went over what I could have done differently, helped me solve the problem, and didn't make me feel bad about it. She was very supportive and understanding and I felt she had my back. She doesn't let people walk over her but she remains approachable and fun to be around.*

The staff also said this manager is always pushing them to be better. Because her feedback to them—both positive and negative—is so clear, people who work with her feel they can be more creative and risk-taking. That's the foundation of a culture of learning and accountability.

If explorers do well, what about the exploders and excusers? Both have limited effectiveness. Bosses who are seen as bullies end up with employees who revert to that dangerous phrase I've warned you about: "Just tell me what you want me to do." Those employees stop making independent decisions and taking risks, for fear of incurring wrath. Or they just leave.

Excusers, in their effort to keep peace in the family, may actually lose the respect of hardworking employees who feel the boss isn't holding everyone to the same performance standards. They can also be seen as protecting their own people while pointing the finger at other departments, building tensions and killing collaboration.

My advice? Be strategic in your response to errors. Base your reactions on three things: the individual employee, the situation, and your desired outcome. Exploring is usually the best path—*but not always.* A skilled explorer may survey a situation and determine that a little exploding or excusing is called for.

The key is this: The explorer knows exactly why playing extreme offense or defense is a good tactic, doing it intentionally.

- When a normally even-tempered boss gets fired up because a serious screwup or misdeed puts people or core values at risk, *employees remember.*
- When a boss with high standards stands up for a staffer whose mistake was abetted by management's own shortcomings, *employees remember.*

And when a promising job candidate walks around asking people what it's like to work around your place, your employees will talk about high standards, not high tension.

As I mentioned way back in chapter 2, when a boss handles our mistakes with a deft touch, we never forget. And when that happens, we are much more likely to learn the right lessons—and feel this way about the boss:

He praises good work and realizes that when people make mistakes or fall short, often just a quiet and gentle word is enough to alert them to their errors. He also understands people very well, realizing that different people need to be dealt with in different ways. His standards are exacting, but he understands that being a decent human being is also of prime importance.

Imagine that. A boss can be a decent human being. That leads us to another very important aspect of your life as a manager: your relationship with your own boss, who may— or may not—be the ideal leader.

It's time to talk about how to be the advocate for yourself and your team in your workplace.

CHAPTER 14

Management Is a Team Sport: How to Manage Your Boss, Your Deputies (and Even Your Stress)

Be honest with me: As you've read this book, you've thought about *your own boss* more than a few times, haven't you? Perhaps it was:

"I sure wish *my* boss would master *that* skill,"

Or:

"*Now* I understand how my manager handles that *so well*."

Actually, I hope your supervisor has been on your mind *throughout* this book, because the talent you develop for managing that individual is as important as every other skill you've studied so far. In fact, you add several degrees of difficulty to your quest to become a great boss if you don't master the art of "managing up."

It isn't always easy. With a Boss from Hell, it can be exhausting. Fortunately, there are many more manageable bosses than hellions. And even so-so supervisors become more effective when their subordinates know how to handle them. So what does it really mean to manage the person who's the boss of you? Take a look:

EIGHT ESSENTIALS OF "MANAGING YOUR BOSS"

1. Knowing your manager's work habits and how to work with—or around—them.

2. Understanding your boss's values and how they align with your own.

3. Communicating in ways your manager is most likely to hear and heed.

4. Disagreeing with your leader as the loyal opposition and not the enemy.

5. Advocating effectively for your team's needs and interests.

6. Incorporating your boss's perspective as you make decisions.

7. Earning the boss's trust through your talent, reliability, and integrity.

8. Building a partnership that makes successes much sweeter and failures nonfatal.

Let me be clear—managing up is different from sucking up. It isn't about being a spineless sycophant. It's about doing the hard work of relationship-building with someone who isn't perfect—but neither are you.

You know by now that I teach from my mistakes—and believe me, I almost blew this whole managing up business, big time. It happened when the general manager who had taken a chance on me was promoted within the company. I didn't care much for the man who was named to replace him—his name was Andy Potos—and Andy wasn't my biggest fan, either. I actually thought about quitting. But the general manager, who knew us both well, offered some wise advice: "Get to know one another. You and Andy are alike in ways you don't yet know and different in ways that can help each other."

So my new boss and I had a blunt talk about our perceptions of one another. We had worked in the same organization, but had never really gone beyond surface conversations. I thought he was a brash and bottom-line-fixated sales guy, and he saw me as a holier-than-thou newsperson, bunkered away in a big silo with my team. I still remember the tension in that talk, but also the revelations as we challenged each other's perceptions. At the end of the conversation, we agreed to give things a try for a year.

Fifteen years later, when Andy retired, we could still laugh about our rocky start and marvel at the partnership we had forged, despite our different styles.

He came from the Vince Lombardi school of leadership. Like the legendary Green Bay Packers coach, he was tough, demanding, competitive, and quick to anger. But we both believed in quality journalism and community service—so we built from there.

I learned that behind his intimidating persona was a quick mind that loved a robust debate with a respected sparring partner. As I earned Andy's trust, I could easily question and challenge him. I could also tease him about his interesting idiosyncrasies—like wearing a jogging suit to work or parking his luxury car on sidewalks when he felt like it, spouting unprintable invective about competitors or critics—and always, always raising the bar. Whatever we accomplished was to be celebrated—and then immediately topped!

From our give-and-take, I learned about confidence in negotiations, how to have tough conversations when necessary, how to think bigger and bolder—and about the whole organization, not just my part of it. I also had the best benefit of all: a boss who shared power and truly believed in me. Long after his retirement, we remain friends, and he's been among my biggest cheerleaders as I wrote this book.

And to think I almost walked away from that opportunity.

Learn from my experience, or heed the words of management gurus John Gabarro and John Kotter. They wrote the now classic *Harvard Business Review* article called "Managing Your Boss," over thirty years ago:

> No doubt some subordinates will resent that on top of all their other duties, they also need to take the time and energy to manage their relationships with their bosses. Such managers fail to realize the importance of this activity and how it can simplify their jobs by eliminating potentially severe problems.

There's a real payoff for you in this. Let me show you the rules of the road when it comes to managing the person who signs your paycheck—or at least keeps it coming!

Rule #1 of Managing Up: It's Your Job to Adapt to Your Boss

Just as your employees know it's not a democracy, you must acknowledge that the partnership with your boss isn't one of true equals. One of you earns more money, gets the final say, controls more resources, and determines your future. We know who that is.

At the same time, one of you may be smarter than the other. That smarter partner might be *you*. It happens. In fact, *maybe that's why your boss hired you.*

My guess is that you're both bright and resourceful—but each in your own ways. Your personalities may vary, along with your work habits and communication styles. Your differences will be far less of a problem if you start with the assumption that it's your responsibility to adapt to your boss's way of doing things.

If your boss isn't the greatest listener, it's up to you to send recap notes after a conversation. If your boss is a long-range thinker, you may have to become a much better planner. If your boss is an extrovert and you're an introvert, you may have to step up your presentation skills so they match the style your manager expects.

Your boss may delegate things to you that you're not crazy about, tell boring stories, or make last-minute requests that interrupt your plans—*because that's what bosses do.*

What *you* do is find the most constructive way to deliver what your boss needs.

Bosses value people who deliver. Not mindlessly or without questions, of course. But the more you build a reputation for reliability, the more credibility you'll have. So, when you differ on truly important issues—not just style points—you can speak truth to power.

RULE #2 OF MANAGING UP: NO SURPRISES

Top bosses may differ in many ways—but they agree on this: they **never want to be blindsided by bad news**. I suspect they wouldn't want to be the last to learn about exceptionally *good* news either, but trust me, that's not what keeps them up at night.

Here are the scenarios they worry about most:

- You delay telling them about a problem, which then explodes into a disaster.
- Their own leaders confront them about an issue that's festering among the troops—and they're clueless about it.
- A key client or customer contacts them with a complaint and they are caught flat-footed—unprepared to respond and unarmed with background information that you could have provided.
- A good employee leaves because of an unresolved issue that could have been addressed, if only the top bosses had known.

While you dutifully try to follow the "no surprises" rule, you face two big challenges:

Knowing your boss's "tell me" triggers. While I've listed a few managerial nightmare scenarios, each boss has a slightly different personal threshold of "need to know."

Your manager may have been burned by some scenario in the past and is now especially vigilant about that subject. Your boss may want you to touch base on anything involving legal issues and everything that costs over a certain dollar amount. Your manager may be micromanaged from above, and therefore leans on you for information about seemingly minor things. Once again, it is up to *you* to learn those "need to know" parameters.

Delivering bad news can be risky. It's easy for me to say, "Alert your boss to trouble," but that early warning may require a confession of your own mistake or—and this is even more dicey—the revelation that *something your boss has done* is causing problems.

If it's your error, be proactive. Own up to it and be prepared to add what you plan to do about it. If it's a misdeed by your staff, take responsibility for whatever piece of the mess is yours and work with your boss on next steps. My boss tended to be an exploder—but I learned that he would quickly shift to explorer mode when people came to him as early as possible about mistakes, were completely candid, and were already working on solutions.

When the early alert is about something your boss is responsible for, present yourself as the "loyal opposition." That is, you aren't an in-house critic and your message isn't, "I told you so!"

Frame your bad news in the spirit of support: "Boss, I think I owe you a heads-up. I know we debated about reduced staffing on Saturdays and you said we have to make it work because of budget. We're five weeks into it, we've made several adjustments, but there are some real quality control issues surfacing and I know you'd want to know now, rather than later."

My advice to you: *When in doubt, inform.* The danger of overcommunicating pales in comparison to the riskiness of violating the "no surprises" rule.

RULE #3 OF MANAGING UP: STAY ON YOUR BOSS'S RADAR

I still remember the first management conference I attended as a newly promoted news director. One of the professional development sessions focused on managing up. The speaker said, "It's your job to speak face-to-face with your general manager *at least once a day.*"

And I thought: "Are you kidding? I have a line of people waiting at my door to talk with me, hours of news to supervise, future planning to take care of, and I'm supposed leave my beloved shop floor to socialize upstairs in carpet land?"

As if reading my mind, the speaker said, "And if you think you're too busy, you are actually neglecting an important part of your work—being an advocate for your staff and yourself." That message struck a chord.

Until then, I naively assumed there were only three reasons to see the top person in the organization: either he called a meeting, or I had a problem too big to handle alone, or I delivered news about something extraordinary.

Mind you, my boss had never told me that. Bosses rarely give you a formal list of their rules of the road. You have to figure them out. Or listen to good advice, as I did. I trained myself to touch base with my boss in the spaces around those three extremes.

You should, too. Work out a rhythm that accommodates

both of your schedules and styles, so it becomes a natural part of your workflow. Talk about ideas, issues, and upcoming projects. Ask how the boss is doing (what a radical thought—checking on the boss's well-being!).

Don't miss opportunities to talk about problems you've solved or opportunities you've seized. When communication is commonplace between you and your boss, it builds context for everything you share. When you highlight a genuine win, you're not bragging, you're just reporting.

In fact, you are actually doing your boss a favor when you give him or her some "feedback fodder." Here's what I mean. When people rise in an organization, two things happen:

1. Their feedback becomes far more important to employees.
2. They have less daily contact with people and product.

So in order to help them meet the challenge, you become their honest broker of information. When you say, "I thought you'd want to know that Paul Nelson came up with the solution to the software glitch that's frustrated everyone—and he did it while working on two other projects. If you have a minute, a word from you would really matter"—you are giving your boss material for the kind of feedback people need and deserve.

If you're still not convinced about the need for continuing connections, just know this: When you're not staying on your boss's radar, other managers take your place.

Top bosses spend their days hearing pitches for ideas and resources—and deciding who gets what. They're also planning long-range strategies and tactics that may involve or affect your team. They may be hearing from the customers or clients or patients or students you serve.

You want them to base their responses and decisions on what they know about you and your team, not what they guess. Your work, and that of your employees, doesn't "speak for itself." You are the voice. Don't be silent while managers of other teams are doing the talking for theirs.

Even in the most collegial, collaborative workplace, there is always a competition for resources and opportunities. Don't give up your share by default—by not making every possible connection with your boss.

Rule #4 of Managing Up: Manage in Your Own Name

If you want to maintain a strong relationship with your boss, don't invoke that person's name whenever you have to deliver unpopular news. It's tempting to say, "*The boss* wants it this way," or "*They* decided to change the rules," but if you do that regularly, you are creating an "us versus them" culture—and you're positioning yourself outside the management team, which is disingenuous. This is especially important when you are giving negative feedback. You can't leave the impression that you're the good cop and your boss is the bad one. Employees see through it. Sooner or later your boss will find out and feel betrayed.

Now, I know you have questions about that. Do I mean you can *never* express disagreement with your boss to the troops? I think you can, especially if you have a very good relationship with your boss and you choose your words carefully. There's a big difference between, "I fought with the boss about this but I got squashed like a bug," and "We had different takes on it. It's not my first choice, but ultimately, this is the way we're going."

If you find that your conscience compels you to put clear distance between your manager's decision and your own strong belief, try to frame it in the most diplomatic terms. This is where your emotional intelligence skills kick in. I suggest you speak as though the boss were right there in the room listening to you: "Cathy and I disagreed about dropping the project. I thought it deserved more funding, and I wish I could have made a better case. In the end, it was her executive decision to make. We'll move forward."

Now, if you find that your conscience tugs at you regularly and painfully, and speaking even neutrally, much less positively about the boss's decisions would make you a hypocrite—then that's another problem. We'll cover it in the Bad Boss section.

Rule #5 of Managing Up: Learn how to pitch an idea so your boss will catch it

Some of our best ideas don't get traction with our bosses because we present them poorly. Think clarity, framing, relevance, timing, and follow-up. Whether your boss likes ideas pitched in person or in writing, these tips should help you.

- **Get to the point.** Try to state your idea in one clear sentence. Use the "elevator pitch" test: Can you state your case in the time it takes for an average elevator ride?

- **Frame your idea positively.** If you start by saying, "Everyone knows we have a problem with...," your manager may hear it as a personal accusation instead of a suggested solution. Try: "I believe I have a way to help...," or "I'd like your input on an idea I've developed..." If you and your boss have already identified a challenge to tackle, then frame it as your shared opportunity: "You know how we've wanted to reduce energy costs? I may have an answer for us."

  And here are three words I recommend you *never say to your boss*:

  "Somebody ought to..."

  It translates to bosses as, "I love to point out problems for other people to fix."

- **Be sensitive to your manager's current challenges and priorities.** What matters most to your boss right now? Hiring challenges? Budget squeeze? New initiatives? The more you know about your manager's current menu, the better you can determine what to add to or help take off the plate. Most important: You can align your idea with the boss's current priorities—or let it rest until it's a better fit.

- **Watch your timing.** Look for low-stress moments to make your pitch. Times to avoid: right after your manager returns from a big meeting and has a backlog of work, monthly report time (or anytime the boss is trying to beat a deadline), after another person has just been in to ask for something, and after any meeting that appeared contentious. Use your powers of observation, the workplace grapevine—and if the boss has an administrative assistant, use the wonderful relationship you've built with that person to get your cues.

- **Know your manager's values.** This is critical to connecting with your manager. If your manager has stated strong core values for your organization, make certain you know them and how your idea supports them. The more closely your idea or issue connects with those values, the greater your chance of achieving managerial buy-in.

- **Be prepared to list benefits and acknowledge challenges.** Bosses appreciate it when you do your homework. If they ask about the cost-benefit ratio of your idea, the benefits you describe should be specific and measurable. Don't try to fuzzy up any potential challenges or wait for your boss to bring them up. Be proactive in acknowledging reasonable questions or concerns about your idea and how you'd address them.

- **Be prepared with a next step.** Your boss may suggest a next step. Be prepared to be a part of it, even if it adds time to a process you'd like to see move more rapidly. If you sense your manager has no next step in mind, be prepared to suggest one—one that's practical and includes the appropriate people in your organization. Good ideas wither away when no one follows through on the step that turns talk into action.

- **Follow up and follow through.** When the light turns green, move! Send a confirming message to your boss that recaps and confirms your decision and next steps. A thank-you is a nice touch, since bosses appreciate positive feedback, too. The best way to make your future pitching even easier is to develop a track record for delivering on a plan or a promise. While others said, "Somebody ought to," you said, "I'll do it"—and you did.

Here's one more tip from my boss, who wasn't one to mince words. He said that too many managers don't know the key rule he learned as a top salesman: When you've made the sale, shut up. If your boss gives you a green light, stop lobbying or you might say something that causes your manager to reconsider! Just go do it!

Testing Your Knowledge About Your Boss

The more you know about your boss, the better you can manage up. That's why I developed a questionnaire to help you determine the depths of your insights into your manager as a boss and as a person. See how many of these questions you can answer.

A few may throw you a curve. That's fine. I hope they push you to learn a lot more about your leader.

CHECK YOURSELF: TWENTY QUESTIONS ABOUT YOUR BOSS

1. **Communication:** How does your boss prefer to *give* information to you? How does your boss prefer to *get* information from you?

---

2. **Face time:** What's the best way to get uninterrupted time with your boss?

---

3. **Meetings:** How would your boss describe an ideal meeting?

---

4. **Problem-solving:** When you're handling a problem, at what point might your boss want to be informed or involved?

---

5. **Pressure points:** What are the greatest pressures your boss is currently facing?

---

6. **Stress management:** How does your boss handle stress and pressure?

---

7. **Organizational reputation:** What is your boss most respected for by his/her bosses?

---

8. **Experience and expertise—greater:** What are your boss's top areas of professional experience and expertise?

---

9. **Experience and expertise—lesser:** What are some areas of your work in which your boss has less experience or training?

(Continued)

10. **Vision:** How would your boss describe his/her vision for your organization, your team, or your work?

_____

11. **Values:** What values does your boss stand for, first and foremost?

_____

12. **Nonnegotiables:** On what matters will your boss never compromise?

_____

13. **Hot buttons:** Does your boss have any pet peeves?

_____

14. **Collaboration:** Looking across the organization and its managers, with whom does your boss work exceptionally well?

_____

15. **Bridge-building:** Are there areas in your organization where your boss has opportunities for better collaboration?

_____

16. **Blind spots:** Does your boss have any blind spots—areas he/she doesn't notice or focus on?

_____

17. **Personal passions:** What are your boss's passions outside of work?

_____

18. **Influences:** Who's the best boss your boss ever worked for?

_____

19. **Great day:** What's a great day at work for your boss?

_____

20. **You:** What does your boss think you do exceptionally well?

_____

How did you do? Were you able to answer most of the questions? When I administer a quiz like this and people miss a few responses, it's possible they haven't worked with a boss long enough to discover the answers. But too often, it's because they haven't made a genuine effort to learn as much as they should about the manager—or didn't know how.

Don't let that be you, because within the answers you'll find opportunities.

For example:

- If you know your boss's current pressures, it can help you set priorities.
- When you know what managers are respected by their own bosses, you know the reputation they want to maintain.
- When you identify your boss's areas of expertise, you can tap that knowledge and understand why he/she might be tempted to micromanage you in those areas.

- If you know where your boss lacks expertise, you can helpfully fill in the gaps.
- If you know the boss's vision and values, it helps you make decisions that support them, and not work at cross-purposes.
- If you know what a boss considers nonnegotiable, you won't waste your time fighting no-win battles.
- If you know your manager's hot buttons, you can train your team not to push them.
- If you know your manager's allies in management, it provides you clues about networking in your organization—and potential partnerships you may build.
- If you know your boss's blind spots, you can be a second set of eyes.
- If you know the boss's passions outside of work, you can find common ground on human terms.
- If you know the best boss your boss ever worked for, you'll gain insights into how your leader defines leadership, and what's expected of you.

Your Next Assignment: Check Your Work!

Why not check your answers with your boss? You can find out how well you know or guessed—and you can fill in some blanks. I've intentionally made the questions as nonjudgmental as possible, so you're not sharing a critique of your manager, just your depth of objective knowledge. (Okay, if you think the one about blind spots might press a hot button, just leave it blank.)

I've done this exercise with countless managers. I've encouraged them to use versions of my "20 Questions" quiz as a springboard to a wide-ranging, in-depth conversation with their supervisors. In more than a few cases, it helped resolve some misunderstandings.

You'll rarely have a better opportunity to gather so much valuable information in one sitting!

But What If You Work for a Really Bad Boss?

You've heard me say that no boss is perfect—and even the great ones disappoint people every day. Sadly, for a select few, disappointing is what they do best. They're people with the title of manager, so you're expected to follow them. But they're not leaders in any sense, so given the choice, you'd go another way—any other way.

What constitutes a truly bad boss? The best analysis I've seen comes from Harvard leadership scholar Barbara Kellerman in her book *Bad Leadership: What It Is, How It Happens, Why It Matters*.

Kellerman lists seven types of bad leadership. The worst bosses may fit into multiple groups:

- **Incompetent:** Lacking the skill or will to sustain effective action
- **Rigid:** Unyielding in opposition to positive change
- **Intemperate:** Lacking in self-control
- **Callous:** Uncaring or unkind to others
- **Corrupt:** Lying, cheating, or stealing
- **Insular:** Minimizing or disregarding the welfare of those outside their circle
- **Evil:** Using pain as an instrument of power and dominance

How do such people stay in power? They may own the business, bamboozle their own bosses, or blind them with great short-term results. Sometimes, the people around them simply choose not to oppose or expose them. They are intimidated or co-opted. They hunker down and avoid contact. Some just flee.

Bad bosses require extreme "managing up" skills. Every situation is different, of course, but here are some survival suggestions:

- Make certain you aren't part of the problem. Keep doing good work in the face of pressure.
- Use your emotional intelligence to respond rationally to irrational behavior.
- Look for mentors and coaches to help you.
- Jump ship if you must, but do it with a plan, not on impulse.

Sometimes you just have to "manage out" a really bad boss:

- Find alliances with other good managers in the organization.
- Keep meticulous records about your boss's performance.
- Talk with HR, especially if you believe the boss's behaviors violate company policy, or are unethical or illegal.
- Get an attorney if the issues are serious and you don't have complete confidence in your company's self-policing systems.

Working to neutralize a boss can be risky but righteous business. The better your track record in the organization, the more credible you will be. I've given you general tips because what you need most is a coach who knows your organization, its policies and procedures, your local employment laws—and how best to help you navigate the challenges.

Just remember, there's a business case to be made for eradicating bad bosses. Stanford's business guru Robert Sutton, whom I've quoted before, calls it the "No Asshole Rule" and wrote a book by the same name. He says:

> Organizations that drive in compassion and drive out fear attract superior talent, have lower turnover costs, share ideas more freely, have less dysfunctional internal competition and trump the external competition.

Maybe if you're really fortunate, you'll get to take the place of a really bad boss. The contrast will be striking and you'll build a following faster than you'd ever dreamed you could. Like this manager:

> *She became our manager a few months back. The manager she replaced wasn't highly respected and that caused morale problems. Those problems have disappeared. She is an excellent manager of people. She brings calmness and a certain sense of cooperative work that's highly refreshing.*

WHAT ABOUT THE MANAGERS WHO REPORT TO (AND MANAGE) YOU?

Choosing and Caring for Your Deputies

We've given a lot of thought to your boss, for good reason. Now it's time to examine your relationship with your deputies—the managers who report to you. I can tell you without hesitation that whatever success I enjoyed as a boss would not have been possible without my extraordinary management team. I could fill several pages describing the joy of working with them—but I can also reduce our secret formula to two words: **talent** and **trust**.

With talent and trust, you and your deputies can tackle any challenge, tell each other anything, and look forward to doing it all again tomorrow! But you must remember that your mid-managers aren't just your "helpers." They are your frontline eyes, ears, brain, and conscience, provided you hire and care for them well.

If you don't have any deputies right now, you probably will down the road. Soon they'll be filling out that 20 Questions sheet, with you as the person under the microscope! Here are my tips for building your own team of rock stars.

TEN TIPS FOR MANAGING YOUR DEPUTIES

1. **Hire for character.** Trust is indeed the lifeblood of good management teams. But it's not enough that *you* trust your managers; the staff must have faith in them, too. It's a

high bar. Vet carefully. Assume *your* reputation is on the line with every managerial hire you make.

2. **Don't hire your clone.** Always look for people who share your core values; that's a given. But beyond that, *don't hire in your own image*. Look for people who bring diversity in every possible way: gender, ethnicity, age, experience, ideas, talent, and personality. Seek out people who are smarter than you, who fill in your knowledge and skill gaps, and who make the whole team stronger.

3. **Hire your replacement.** The boss who hired me said, "You should be able to look out your door and see your replacement." Have the wisdom and self-confidence to hire people who could take your job right now, or in the near future. Grooming people for greatness doesn't put you at risk; it can make you more valuable. Remember, if you hire people of character (See Tip #1), they wouldn't use their growing success to depose their leader.

4. **Look for rising stars from within.** Some of my best managers were promoted by popular demand. Listen to your staff, especially your highest-performing and most collaborative employees. If they advocate for an internal candidate and have the facts to support their position, give their advice extra weight. If the rising star is a good fit for the opening, he or she will have a built-in cheering section from the start.

5. **Don't become insular.** As rewarding as it can be to promote from within, don't completely wall yourself off from outsiders. It may be faster and cheaper to elevate managers from within, but people who've worked in the same place together for some time may develop tunnel vision. They may think things ain't broke and don't need fixing, when a less invested person may inspire innovation. But "outsider" status

isn't enough. It has to be "outsider with valuable experience and ideas." After hiring an "outsider," by all means cease using the term.

6. **Share power.** You knew I was going to say this, didn't you? If you give your mid-level managers responsibility, you'd better give them authority, too. Top-performing management teams have a shared understanding of the authority each person has to make decisions independently. When you're not a micromanager or a fixer, they know to turn to you on major policy, personnel, or budget issues, but are free to make important daily judgment calls by themselves.

7. **Share information.** Your assistants can't operate at maximum effectiveness unless you share strategic plans, market research, budget data, and performance metrics. Remember, you've hired people of character (See Tip #1, yet again). Give them the goods to make informed decisions.

8. **Encourage—and endure—candid feedback.** Mid-level managers are closer to the front lines than you are. They should be your early warning system when the troops are unsettled or when a system is flawed. They should be unafraid to tell you if you're about to do something unwise— or you already did!

9. **Share the credit AND the blame.** We live in a world that shines the spotlight on the top leader. Widen the beam at every opportunity. When there's a success, credit your co-leaders. Make it absolutely clear when their ideas, solutions, or just plain hard work are the driving force behind wins and wise moves. When they mess up, stand with them and take your lumps. Then work together to find solutions.

10. **Help them soar.** High achievers need to know they're not stagnating. They need stretch assignments, learning

opportunities, and the opportunity to become experts in a meaningful subject area—in other words, all the intrinsic motivators you can fuel. And though this can be tough, you must support them even if their next big professional step leads them away from your team.

One valuable member of my management team had a dream of one day teaching at the college level. We crafted a schedule that allowed him to work on his master's degree while working full-time. That accommodation, which went on for several years, was more than repaid by his dedication and work ethic throughout, and by the thrill it gave everyone when he reached his goal.

You don't keep high-quality deputies by chaining them to their desks. If their next big opportunity presents itself outside your organization, help them negotiate that career move wisely—and throw them a great farewell celebration.

Every Manager Needs a Safe Venting Zone

Now that I've encouraged you to manage your boss and your deputies, I want to say a word about managing another on-the-job companion—your stress. Being a great boss is hard work. Some days are harder than others, courtesy of bosses who do you wrong, staffers who let you down, or colleagues who tick you off.

That's when you want to let off some steam. You want to validate your victimhood and confirm that your indignation is righteous.

Great bosses know that even blowing off steam needs to

be done strategically or it can be self-defeating. In fact, it can be self-destructive if you break the cardinal rule of complaining: Don't vent to your employees.

They might be close by, a cheering audience, with sympathetic ears—but don't do it! It's as unwise as taking out a full-page newspaper ad to list your grievances. Your words become part of the public record. They also become great fodder for gossip. Long after you've cooled down or moved on, your old quotes are out there somewhere, haunting you. That's the price you pay for venting in the wrong zone. It's why I believe every manager needs a "Safe Venting Zone."

Used properly, your Safe Venting Zone provides you with ideas, solutions, and a little therapy. In the Zone, you are away from your staff and in the company of a highly qualified partner. To measure up to the task, your "Official Safe Venting Zone Partner" should be:

- A smart manager who understands the responsibilities of leadership
- A person who knows your strengths and weaknesses and still likes you
- A person who keeps confidences
- A person who knows when you simply need to complain—or when you should turn that talk into action
- A person who is equally willing to hold your hand or kick your butt—and who instinctively understands when to employ either response
- A good coach who helps you plan your next steps

What if you don't have a partner like this in your workplace? I'd advise you to reach out to a former boss, mentor, or colleague. The disadvantage is that these folks won't know the nuances of your organization and may be *too* biased in your favor to challenge your perceptions. But if that's the best you have, go for it.

At the same time, I'd encourage you to look inward. What could you be doing to build a Safe Venting Zone relationship at work—one in which *you* are the leader another manager turns to for talk, truth, and trust?

Truth and trust: just the right words to lead us to our last, most important pages together—and what really sets great bosses apart from all the rest.

CHAPTER 15

For Great Bosses, It's Always About the Values

As we begin our final chapter together, let me thank you for the hard work you've done thus far. Thanks for taking quizzes, filling out worksheets, and thinking deeply about what it means to be a top-notch manager. But there's still work to do. I have another question for you to answer, one I've reserved for this moment. I'd like you to look far forward in time, to your legacy as a leader. My question is this:

What do you *really* want to be known for?

Perhaps it will be for efficiency and effectiveness, for smart strategies and innovation, for launching the careers of good people—or for being wildly successful in the profession you love.

Those are wonderful aspirations. But I hope you aim higher.

When your story is told, I hope your reputation will have been built on **values**. I hope that whenever people talk about your accomplishments, they will speak not only of *what you've done*, but also the *person you are* and *what you stand for*. That's true leadership.

It's why I saved some very important ideas for our last pages together. I want to focus on the values and qualities that distinguish the most positive workplace cultures and also the bosses who lead them. We'll examine three key differentiators:

- **Integrity**
- **Humanity**
- **Levity**

Integrity and humanity may not surprise you—but levity? Yes, don't laugh, Actually, please *do* laugh. It's important—and I've reserved fun and laughter for the last of our lessons on this leadership journey. I want you to finish *Work Happy* with a lasting and contagious smile.

But first, we'll focus on the most serious subject of all, and why it is at the core of management and leadership. I'm talking about your ethical compass: Integrity.

The Value of Integrity: It's Not Just About the Rules

When I first became a manager, I thought I understood the scope of my duties when it came to keeping my team on the straight and narrow. I believed it was my responsibility to know and enforce:

- The company's rules and guidelines
- Federal, state, and local laws about the workplace and our work
- Professional codes of ethics

That was another one of my mistakes. Reread what I just wrote and see if you can spot what I got wrong. Go ahead, I'll wait.

Puzzled? If you didn't catch my error, it's probably because you focused only on the bullet points about rules, laws, and codes of ethics. They're just fine. The mistake was my narrow assumption that the presence of a boss who "knows and enforces" the rules is the best path to virtuous behavior in organizations. It's like appointing yourself to be a one-person integrity squad.

There's much more to leadership and integrity than being the smartest sheriff in town.

Remember back in chapter 3 when we plugged into the Power Grid of Leadership and its **referent power**? That's the type of power that causes people to identify with you and what you stand for. They're not *afraid* of you; they want to learn from you and emulate the best of what you do.

Here's the bottom line: Bosses with referent power don't simply memorize and enforce the rules; they develop workplace cultures in which **employees share a deep understanding of the values that guide them**. Staffers feel competent about that knowledge, confident in making good decisions, and committed to doing the right thing.

Employees at all levels of the organization talk openly and often about ethics and standards, rules and laws. But the framework of the conversation isn't:

"Don't you dare screw up and put the company at risk, or you'll suffer the consequences!"

Instead, it's:

"Knowing who we are and what we stand for, what's the best way to handle this?"

The negative, "Don't you dare screw up" mindset is what Lynn S. Paine, a Harvard business ethicist, describes as a **compliance-based** approach to ethical conduct.

In compliance cultures, prevention, detection, and punishment are paramount. The basic compliance script is this: Lay down the rules, have employees sign statements saying they've read the company handbook, monitor people closely, and threaten them with sanctions. It's based on the notion that the biggest threat to organizations is some rogue employee in the ranks, and the compliance approach will neutralize the occasional troublemaker.

But Paine, writing in the *Harvard Business Review*, poked holes in that logic:

Rarely do the character flaws of a lone actor fully explain corporate misconduct. More typically, unethical business practice involves the tacit, if not explicit, cooperation of others and reflects the values, attitudes, beliefs, language and behavioral patterns that define an organization's operating culture.

In other words, bad apples are often a function of bad barrels. And managers create those barrels: the everyday workplace culture.

Professor Paine argues that instead of merely demanding compliance, organizations and managers take an **integrity-based** approach, and I wholeheartedly agree. How does it differ from compliance? Integrity cultures start with the assumption that rules and their enforcement are indeed very important in the workplace—but that **values** need to be embedded in the organization's strategy, its systems, and in every possible aspect of the daily work.

As a manager who wants to build a culture of integrity, you can start exactly where I did—knowing the rules and knowing your job is to enforce them—but then go on to do much more.

Find what I call "points of entry"—opportunities to talk about core values—from job candidate interviews to goal-setting meetings to employee feedback to problem-solving to resource allocation to chitchat around the coffee machine.

It's an extension of the "feedback glasses" concept you mastered in chapter 9. Since you're already on the lookout for opportunities to provide feedback, you simply find ways to incorporate what you stand for into those conversations. Your feedback isn't framed around not getting sued, audited, or fined, losing money or being politically correct; it's about quality, service, safety, fairness, and corporate citizenship.

In integrity cultures, employees aren't focused on a fear of being caught doing something wrong; they're proud of how clearly people believe in doing things right. They are less cynical than their counterparts in compliance cultures, who often feel that the real focus of the vigilance is to provide cover for the topmost bosses, so if things go wrong the rank and file will take the fall.

So by all means build and nurture a culture of integrity. It's a lot easier to be a smart sheriff when everyone on your staff is a smart deputy. Here are some tips to make it all happen:

Six Tips for Building a Culture of Integrity

1. Ethical decision-making is more than knowing right from wrong and using common sense.

There are some bosses who think developing or using written standards and guidelines isn't really necessary. They believe in keeping things simple. After all, we already have a Golden Rule, Ten Commandments, and the Boy and Girl Scout creeds—that should cover us, right?

But ethical decision-making is a complex process that goes beyond mottos and pledges. It involves balancing competing pressures and loyalties. When is a gift a friendly gesture and when is it a bribe? When might an employee's off-the-job conduct, like posting on social media, potentially affect the workplace? If an employee feels harassed by bosses or coworkers, what should that person do? If workers believe a respected colleague has a substance abuse problem, to whom do they turn?

Relying on your gut instinct alone isn't enough. Having

guidelines *and* a shared, understood decision-making process creates better outcomes and stronger cultures.

2. Written codes of conduct are a good start—if you build on them.

By all means put your standards, practices, and values in writing. Invest in training on ethics, diversity, safety, and legal standards. But don't assume training and handbooks are enough. Remember, the Enron Corporation had a Code of Ethics, even as its leaders broke laws. Rupert Murdoch's News Corporation had a Standards of Business Conduct for its companies, even as its newspaper, the *News of the World*, was embroiled in a major phone hacking scandal in the United Kingdom. It's *all just paper, all just talk*, unless leaders at every level of organizations make the words matter.

Codes are easily overshadowed by *cues*, given out every day by supervisors. If those cues reinforce and reward the wrong things, codes are rendered meaningless. It's up to you to walk the talk, every day. And on training day, learn alongside your employees, even if it's material you've heard before. They get the wrong cue when the boss skips ethics class.

3. What you measure is what you value.

Among the strongest cues leaders give employees are the metrics they use for success. When organizations make diversity a value, they measure how effectively managers recruit or mentor people who've been traditionally underrepresented in the company's ranks. They'll be able to prove—with hard data—whether they've made progress and how they did it.

It's the difference between having "we're an equal opportunity employer" as a slogan and building it into the systems and culture.

When companies make the environment or safety or community service a value, they make it a point to audit those efforts. It isn't just to have a nice story to tell in the annual report—it's an alert to everyone in the organization that just as expenses and revenues are watched with care, so too are core values.

4. When it comes to values, don't play favorites.

I've told you throughout this book that you shouldn't treat everyone alike—and that you can play favorites. But let me be clear: That philosophy applies to communication, motivation, assignments, rewards—but **never to values. No one is exempt from doing the right thing, legally, ethically, or morally**.

I say this because some managers tread too lightly with veteran employees or superstars. They may assume those staffers don't warrant the normal check-and-balance process or they may fear pushback from prima donnas or bullies. Whether it's about conflicts of interest or treating people with civility or turning in accurate, signed expense reports, values and standards aren't discretionary. No one earns the right to bypass integrity. Everyone, including (and especially) the boss, should play by the same rules.

5. Watch out for mixed messages.

Just as you can't bury people in work and then wonder why they don't collaborate on other people's projects, dissonance also pops up when it comes to ethics. A big push for economy or efficiency, as needed as it might be, can be mistaken for a suspension of values if you're not careful.

There are times when you must ask people to do things faster or more cheaply. It's imperative that you work with your team to identify the potential risks involved *before* you run into problems and not dismiss early concerns as overreactions.

This is really a core part of the change management skills you've already studied—learning how to help people adapt to new ways of doing things. In times of change, people often respond with worst-case scenario predictions. Bosses who lead cultures of integrity work with their people to determine what's a false alarm—and what's a true alarm. They develop safeguards so that faster won't trump accuracy and cheaper won't jeopardize safety.

6. When things go wrong (and they will), look at systems, people, and lessons.

Here's another one of the harsh realities of management life. At some point in your career, even if you've built a wonderful culture, you'll find yourself dealing with a mistake or a misdeed that truly disappoints you. Don't let it defeat you. Be the explorer. Do a rigorous analysis of your systems, training, and communication. Fix what's broken.

If your systems are fine but what's flawed is an employee's character, then act decisively to eliminate that danger to your team's integrity. Firing people is never easy, but when you've documented serious misconduct, it is your responsibility to act.

The final step in a tough situation like this is to be as transparent as possible about it. Don't bury big mistakes; learn and teach from them. Those stories are powerful leadership tools.

During one workshop I led for national managers of a major corporation, their new chief executive sat in for the full day. He took part in every exercise. When we focused on sustaining a culture of integrity, he reinforced my teaching with a short but powerful anecdote. He said that when he took over the division, he dismissed an employee known for bringing in significant revenue to the company. The exec didn't name names. He just said that the rainmaker was operating outside the company's values—and that short-term profits could never be allowed to threaten long-term integrity. Period.

In that moment, he let everyone know what he measured, what he valued, and what he really wanted to be known for. All with one simple story.

As a leader, what are the stories you might tell—and what kind of stories will be told about you? It's a great way to lead into our next value: humanity.

THE VALUE OF HUMANITY: CAN YOUR STAFF BE "THE REAL ME" AT WORK?

Here's an assignment: Show me a picture that represents "the real you." Think carefully. You can choose only one. It can be anything you want. What would that picture look like?

Would it be:

- A shot of you on the job, or at a professional function?
- A portrait of you with loved ones or good friends?

- An image featuring you and your pet, your hobby, or a favorite vacation spot?

I'm pretty sure I know which categories you'd be most likely to choose, because I often start a management seminar with this "Real Me" exercise, using pictures submitted by the participants.

We learn quite a bit from those photos. The stories behind the snapshots are often as touching as they are telling. I've seen grandparents whose work ethic inspired generations in a family, learned about cancer survivors, award-winning offspring, spouses and partners who put up with the crazy demands of the managers they love, and some amazing talents that people unleash in their free time.

Think about that. These are bosses who care about their work—in fact, many are absolutely crazy about it. But in their "Real Me" imagery, they choose to demonstrate that they aren't defined by their professional passion alone.

It's more than a fun icebreaker. It's the first lesson I like to teach about leadership: the importance of understanding what people value in their lives—and learning that there's so much more to them than what we might see on the surface.

So, bosses, this leads me to ask you:

- Do you know the "Real Me" of the people who report to you?
- How much of the "Real Me" can they share at work?

The answers to those questions are very important. They can help ascertain a core value of your workplace culture and its leadership:

Do you value **humanity**? Or are your people merely headcount?

You know where I stand on this: Never treat an employee as though he or she is simply headcount, an interchangeable, easily replaceable number on a budget line. Never leave them feeling that the terms "professional" and "personal" are polar opposites.

Don't be this manager:

> *I have been working for the same boss for more than two years and he still doesn't know the names of either of my children. His only interest is that I show up for work and do my job.*

That discouraging quote came from the survey I did a few years back on the subject of work-life balance. It helped shape my thinking on the subject—right down to challenging the term "work-life balance" itself. I developed this new take on the topic:

> Stop thinking and speaking in terms of **work-life balance**. Strive instead for something realistic and achievable: **work-life harmony**.

I say that as a working mom as well as a teacher of management and leadership. I say it to help managers who are wrestling with the subject in their own lives and who want to do whatever they can to respect the humanity of their employees.

Words matter. And the word "balance" inevitably sets us

up to feel like failures. It suggests a scorecard with a fifty-fifty split. For every forty hours of work there should be forty hours to do anything else we want. For every three days spent on an out-of-town assignment, there must be three days of camping with the family. You get my point. It's never that tidy. Our work and home lives are rarely, if ever, in *balance*.

Words matter. And the word "harmony" may help both employees and bosses to not just feel better about work, but take a far more humanistic approach to it. Harmony suggests that the complex demands of our work lives and our personal lives may indeed compete for the limited hours in our days, but they are not necessarily mortal enemies.

Many times, they complement each other. Our jobs, even demanding ones, provide us satisfaction and fulfillment. They are a part of who we are. At the same time, I really believe the experiences of our personal lives can make us more valuable in our careers.

Each of us brings a set of gifts to the workplace, professionally and personally. We bring a few challenges, too. If bosses care more about humanity than headcount, they do whatever they can to build cultures that value harmony and happiness in the workplace.

Here's what that looks like in the real world:

- Employees don't have to check their personal lives and interests at the office door.
- Managers have a pretty good idea what their employees' "Real Me" photos might feature.
- Managers might be happy workaholics, as some are, but they don't demand that everyone else imitate them.

- Managers make certain that extra work and long hours are driven by the normal ebb and flow of business, not by their bad planning, scheduling, or systems.
- Managers aren't social workers or therapists, but they respond with care in times of crisis.
- Managers say, "Go, we'll be fine" when employees feel the call of duty on the home front, for reasons that are wonderful or terrible.

I've already told you that employees will never forget your response during critical moments in their lives. They also remember when the boss is the reason their everyday work-life harmony is way out of tune.

Read these three quotes about bosses and promise me you'll never let this be said about you:

Our requests for time off don't get approved or denied in a timely manner. Sometimes I don't get a reply for a month. It's very difficult to plan a life outside work that way.

And:

I work in a male-dominated office where they believe that picking up sick kids or leaving early to pick up a relative from the airport is a wife's job.

And:

My boss doesn't control the workflow (i.e., set expectations/enforce deadlines) and lets it careen out of control each day.

Every one of those issues chips away at work-life harmony. Every one of them is a preventable management failure. Each one suggests that humanity isn't much of a value in the eyes of those bosses.

I know you want to be better than that. So let me share a few tips with you.

Tips for Humanity and Harmony

1. Be at your best when people face their worst challenges.

When your staffers tell stories of a critical moment in their lives—illness, childbirth, divorce, bereavement—a chapter of that story will very likely deal with the impact on their job. When they talk about your role in that drama, how will they describe you? Will you be a hero, a villain, or some extra on the sidelines who played no real part at all?

2. Support people's celebrations of life's happiest rites and rituals.

We've covered this ground before, but I can't say it often enough. Never miss a chance to cheer for your home team. Help make their good memories even better.

I'll share one of my favorite personal stories about doing just that. One year, a terrific reporter on my team was unable to attend the annual Press Club banquet, though he had won several of the reporting awards to be presented that night. He had a slight scheduling conflict; it was his wedding day. So my boss and I conspired to give him the best of both celebrations. We hired a limousine to make a lightning-fast pickup at his reception, which was not far from the banquet. Imagine the reaction when the banquet emcee announced his awards, and introduced "Mr. *and Mrs.* Charles Benson." The newlyweds entered, arm in arm, in tux and gown. The room erupted in surprised laughter and cheers. The bridal couple graciously accepted both the applause and the awards, and was back on the dance floor at their reception moments later.

Not every gesture of support needs to be quite so flamboyant. A nice note is always welcome, but every now and then it's fun to make a *big* statement, too!

3. Remember that your praise defines the team's priorities; don't send mixed messages.

This one is kind of tricky, so stick with me. I've learned over the years that bosses often tell staff that they support work-life harmony and really mean it—but then inadvertently send contradictory cues. It happens during earnest, positive public feedback. Like this:

> "A big thanks to Maria, who rescheduled her vacation so we could make deadline. That's true dedication."

Those nice words can be heard by other employees as, "I judge people by how willing they are to ditch their personal lives for me." You may not mean it that way, but it's what they may infer.

The solution isn't to stop thanking people—it's to do a better job of embedding your values into your public praise:

"A big thanks to Maria, who rescheduled her vacation so we could make deadline. It was over and above the call of duty and, I hope, the first and last time you'll ever do it. Please thank your husband, Bob, too."

In the second kudos, your appreciation makes it clear that this was indeed a sacrifice and not the norm. And, you thoughtful boss, you even acknowledged her spouse!

4. Don't pit the single against the married, or the childless against the parents.

Work-life harmony is important to all employees. Don't assume that the young, the single, or the childless on your staff should carry a disproportionate burden when it comes to scheduling. Sometimes they do, in fact, volunteer to cover for coworkers, but their kind gesture shouldn't turn into expectations.

And here's a jaw-dropper: I've even heard stories from gay employees about bosses who assume they're good candidates to cover shifts on holidays, so that "family" people can have the time off. Promise me you'll never be that boss!

5. Create a climate where people look out for each other.

When you make humanity a value in your workplace culture, it can go viral. It's up to you to set the tone, and a leader can truly make a difference. I have to give credit for this idea to a highly regarded journalist, Tom Bettag, who was executive producer of ABC's *Nightline* when it was anchored by

Ted Koppel. At one of our leadership seminars, Bettag told us when he took that job, the staff had suffered from a high degree of burnout and turnover. Even though people loved the program and their profession, the relentless "all hands on deck," 24/7 schedule took too much of a toll on their personal lives.

So Bettag told them his philosophy: "Our relationships don't fail because of the long hours we work. It's because of the promises we break to people who care about us." He asked the staff to always look out for each other, so people could make and keep their promises, and he would do his part as well. People still worked hard, but not impossibly so. He must have built one heck of a culture. When Bettag left *Nightline* fourteen years later, his team of thirty-five people presented him with a gift he cherishes—a picture book called "The Children of Nightline." It features portraits of the forty-one offspring born to staff members during his tenure as their boss.

The right leadership, values, and systems make it easier for people to look out for each other. When employees know what's expected of them, when they feel that people share the load, when they are cross-trained and can cover for each other, and when they believe you trust and support them, they self-manage some of the scheduling challenges that would otherwise wind up on your desk.

🌙

In today's economy our workplaces may be running leaner than ever. All the more reason that when it comes to work-life harmony, they shouldn't be meaner, right? In fact, I think it's all the more reason for the last of the values—levity. Also known as just plain fun, it turns "work happy" into a reality, not just a slogan.

The Value of Levity: Let's Get Some Work Done, Just for the Fun of It

I have a bias for laughter. I love the sound of it in the workplace. I can't imagine teaching a single class, much less a seminar, without it. I believe humor is inextricably linked to humanity and harmony—and elevates all of our efforts. If you must know, my husband and I were even married by a Jesuit priest who teaches a college course on the philosophy of humor, moonlights as a clown, and makes exquisite balloon animals.

I'm so serious about levity that I teach it as a value.

I'd like to think there aren't many bosses out there who are deeply biased *against* laughter and levity. I'd rather think of them as *humor-impaired*. They may be those extreme planner personality types I told you about in chapter 7 who are inclined to think that play should begin when the work is finished. Or they are managers who've yet to learn the business case for on-the-job laughing.

So I'll make it for them now—and for you, too.

Researchers who have investigated the impact of humor and fun in the workplace have found it can deliver some powerful payoffs. Humor and fun at work can improve:

- Team-building
- Communication
- Job satisfaction

- Creativity
- Productivity
- Positive workplace culture
- Leadership performance

Notice that last point? Levity can even make you a better leader. The authors of *Executive EQ: Emotional Intelligence in Leadership and Organizations* explain it this way:

> Studies show that a quick infusion of lightheartedness does more than boost your energy. It encourages intuitive flow, makes you more helpful toward others, and significantly improves intelligence processes such as judgment, problem solving, and decision-making when you are facing difficult challenges. It is a great aid to creative transformation.

What if *your* creative transformation involves infusing a little more levity into life at work? How should you go about doing it? I suggest you start with a genuine smile and these five tips:

Lighten Up! Five Tips About Leadership and Fun at Work

1. It starts with you; be a good sport.

Sometimes, the most fun people can have at work is laughing at the boss. Poking fun at powerful people is a staple of classic comedy, from the Three Stooges to Jon Stewart.

Don't assume it's a mutiny because someone does a

dead-on impression of your speaking style, writes a parody of a memo you've written, or tells jokes about some lame mistake you made. I say this with great conviction because I did *all* of those things as an employee, with no intent of sabotaging my bosses. And do you know how they responded? They promoted me to management. (Maybe that was their ultimate revenge!)

Laugh with your team. Let them laugh at you. One of the greatest dividends for being a leader known for quality, integrity, and humanity is that *everyone* can enjoy it when you're the butt of a joke, yourself included.

2. You don't define fun; your employees do.

You knew I couldn't get through a whole book on bosses without some reference to the TV show *The Office*, right? I've waited for just this moment, to share the immortal words of Michael Scott to his long-suffering staff:

> "We're all participating in mandatory fun activities. Funtivities!"

I'm sure you bear no resemblance to the maladjusted manager of Dunder Mifflin, but there's a lesson in his inept attempt to orchestrate workplace levity. When bosses script or schedule fun on their terms, it can be just another top-down assignment—and it can fail miserably.

Mirth works best when it is staff-generated or staff-approved. If you know your staff well enough, you'll have a good sense of how they like to play as well as work. Don't impose athletic competitions or gift swaps or skit productions;

check in with your team before assuming that a good time will be had by all.

3. Cultivate the catalysts of fun on your crew.

Most workplaces are blessed to have some people on staff who can make the place brighter just by showing up. Because of their particular brand of emotional intelligence, they know when stress needs to be knocked back with a shot of laughter and when people need a word of encouragement. They know how to tell a joke and take a joke. They can tease without venom—and are the standard bearers for happiness at work.

If these staffers are class acts as well as class clowns—that is, they're good at their daily work as well as catalysts for fun—then your job as a boss is to let them know how valuable they are. It's especially the case if humor isn't your forte—and let's face it, some perfectly fine folks don't happen to have a well-developed funny bone. So be wise enough to take cues from your levity leaders.

At the same time, always be on the lookout for untapped talent when it comes to fun. We often turn automatically to the same extroverts, because they're so obvious. Meanwhile, there may be other, quieter, but immensely clever people on your staff who have creative ideas about celebrations or surprises.

4. When in doubt, add food.

Let me direct you to the words of culinary legend James Beard, who said:

"Food is our common ground, a universal experience."

Or better yet, that leadership icon Homer Simpson:

"Donuts: Is there anything they can't do?"

Food fuels fun. It brings us together. If you'd like more people to take advantage of your open-door policy, keep a dish of candy on your desk. My tough-as-nails boss always kept an obscenely large stash of mini-sized chocolate bars in a jar for all to share. He took particular delight in distributing them by giant handfuls to the visiting children of employees. My young sons planned ahead and wore cargo pants with huge pockets when they visited Mom at work!

Don't sweat it if budget cuts may have made it hard for you to underwrite frequent celebratory cakes and pizza breaks. A "pot luck" mindset can evolve fairly easily in its place. It usually starts with the boss telling people honestly that the budget's tight and their ideas are welcome. For good measure, you offer to make, bake, or buy something yourself. Your candor and example set the table for it to happen. Soon, people stop mourning the catered days of yore and begin cooking up their own fun.

5. You don't mandate fun; you welcome and reward it so that it grows naturally.

How did Southwest Airlines build a reputation for service with a generous helping of spontaneity and laughter? Its early leaders, Herb Kelleher and Colleen Barrett, set the tone. In fact, her informal title was "Chairman of Fun." Levity became a cornerstone value of the Southwest culture. Employees were rewarded for providing positive and upbeat experiences for customers—and coworkers.

Southwest's execs may be legendary, but my personal hero when it comes to building a culture of fun is the former president of the Poynter Institute, Jim Naughton. He was an extraordinary journalist who lured me from leading a newsroom to leading a classroom. He brought just the right mix of gravitas and "goofytas" to his position as an academic leader.

Because he thought his office was too formal, he installed a pool table for employees and students to enjoy. It sat beside his collection of crazy costume hats, which he loaned out to any seminar participant who cared to assume the identity of a Swami, Construction Worker, Viking, Cheesehead, or Albert Einstein for a day. He played—and was the victim of—more pranks than any one man I know, jokes that were always wickedly creative but never cruel. And he did it all in the name of leadership and laughter, something he teaches to any manager who'll listen. In his words:

> "Fun matters. Fun makes up for modest pay. It takes the sting out of disappointment. It facilitates collaboration. It serves the interests of retention."

In retirement, Jim Naughton still smiled, even as he dealt with the deadly serious challenge of cancer. On the last day of a series of radiation treatments, with naughty glee, he surprised the clinic staff by showing up in a sumo wrestler costume, saying, "Look what your radiation has done to me!" In a book he wrote about his life as a serial prankster and his devotion to levity in good times and in bad, he ended with these words:

As long as I am able, I plan to laugh death in the face.

We lost Jim in August of 2012. The headline of his obituary in the *New York Times* described him as "Newsman and Puckish Inspiration." *Work Happy* had just been released, and I was honored to read from this chapter at his service. There were tears aplenty as people shared stories of Jim's talent, kindness, and hijinks, but an abundance of belly laughs as well—just as he would have wanted.

Your Leadership Legacy

For each one of us who aspires to be a great boss, to be a true leader, it all comes back to that one question, doesn't it?

What do you really want to be known for?

I'm confident you have a very good answer to that question. Why? Because you wouldn't have spent page after page with me, doing the writing and thinking I've asked of you, unless something important within wasn't already guiding you.

I think you already knew that the most important thing leaders do is to help others succeed and to be happy in their work. I think you wanted to find more joy in the joyful parts of management and learn to better roll with the challenges— and that's why you've gone the distance with me.

I suspect you've already served separation papers on your Evil Twin, that you're looking spiffy in your feedback glasses, that you're helping rev up someone's Big Mo, and that you've even started sitting on your hands. You and I know what all that means, don't we? It means you're not just self-aware; you're now determined to manage yourself so you can truly lead others. You're on a quest to build a culture where people are proud and happy to come to work.

You're preparing for that day when someone like me hands you a manila folder, filled with feedback from your team. You'll be nervous, because that's normal. You'll open the folder and begin to read. And there it will be, the message you hoped to see.

They will say you are a great boss.

Congratulations. You've made work happy.

Resources

I mentioned many good researchers and writers in this book, whose thinking helps shape my teaching. In case you'd like to read more, I've listed these resources for you.

Chapter 1: The Challenges and Joys of Management—a Reality Check

Joel Brockner, "Why It's So Hard to Be Fair," http://hbr.org/2006/03/why-its-so-hard-to-be-fair/ar/1http://www4.gsb.columbia.edu/cbs-directory/detail/494882/Brockner.

Daniel Ames, "What Breaks a Leader: The Curvilinear Relation Between Assertiveness and Leadership" (PDF of article attached in linked article), http://www.apa.org/news/press/releases/2007/02/good-leaders.aspx.

Edgar H. Schein, *The Corporate Culture Survival Guide*, new and rev. ed. (San Francisco: Jossey-Bass, 2009). A short biography of Schein is available at http://mitsloan.mit.edu/faculty/detail.php?in_spseqno=121&co_list=f.

Chapter 2: What Employees Never Forget—and Never Forgive (and Why They Don't Like Your Evil Twin)

Roderick M. Kramer and Tom R. Tyler, *Trust in Organizations: Frontiers of Theory and Research* (Thousand Oaks, CA: Sage Publications, 1996). See especially pp. 116–17.

Chapter 3: How to Tap the Power Grid of Leadership

John R. P. French and Bertram Raven, "Bases of Social Power," in Dorwin Cartwright, ed., *Studies in Social Power* (Ann Arbor: University of Michigan Press, 1959).

Robert I. Sutton, *Good Boss, Bad Boss: How to Be the Best... and Learn from the Worst* (New York: Basic Books, 2010).

Niccolò Machiavelli, *The Prince* (1513).

John P. Kotter, "What Leaders Really Do," *Harvard Business Review*, May-June 1990.

Warren Bennis and Joan Goldsmith, *Learning to Lead: A Workbook on Becoming a Leader* (New York: Basic Books, 2003).

Joseph C. Rost, *Leadership for the Twenty-First Century* (Westport, CT: Greenwood, 1993).

Chapter 4: Manage Yourself, So You Can Lead Others

Linda A. Hill, *Becoming a Manager: How New Managers Master the Challenges of Leadership* (Boston: Harvard Business School Publishing, 2003).

Jeffrey Zaslow, "Sully's Remarkable Journey and What We Can Learn from It," *Wall Street Journal*, October 14, 2009, http://online.wsj.com/article/SB10001424052748703790404 574469160016077646.html.

Chesley Sullenberger with Jeffrey Zaslow, *Highest Duty: My Search for What Really Matters* (New York: William Morrow, 2009).

"What I Got Back," *Parade*, October 11, 2009, http://www .parade.com/news/2009/10/11-what-i-got-back.html.

Daniel Goleman, Richard Boyatzis, and Annie McKee, *Primal Leadership: Realizing the Power of Emotional Intelligence* (Boston: Harvard Business School Publishing, 2002).

Carolyn Butler, "Researchers Ask Why Optimism Is Associated with Health, Pessimism with Disease," *Washington Post*, January 12, 2010, http://www.washingtonpost.com/ wp-dyn/content/article/2010/01/11/AR2010011103365.html.

"Managing Emotions in the Workplace: Do Positive and Negative Attitudes Drive Performance?," Knowledge@Wharton, http://knowledge.wharton.upenn.edu/article.cfm?articleid =1708.

CHAPTER 5: You and Your Big Mouth: Communication Tips and Traps

Charles Conrad and Marshall Scott Poole, *Strategic Organizational Communication: In a Global Economy*, 6th ed. (Stamford, CT: Wadsworth Publishing, 2004).

Gail T. Fairhurst and Robert A. Sarr, *The Art of Framing: Mastering the Language of Leadership* (San Francisco: Jossey-Bass, 1996).

Arky Ciancutti and Thomas L. Steding, *Built on Trust: Gaining*

Competitive Advantage in Any Organization (New York: McGraw-Hill, 2000).

Chapter 6: To Win the Battle for Your Time, Talk Back to the Voices in Your Head

Benedict Carey, "Feel Like a Fraud? At Times, Maybe You Should," *New York Times*, February 5, 2008, http://www.nytimes.com/2008/02/05/health/05mind.html.

Lucas Laursen, "No, You're Not an Impostor," *Science*, February 15, 2008, http://sciencecareers.sciencemag.org/career_development/previous_issues/articles/2008_02_15/caredit_a0800025.

Karen Kaplan, "Unmasking the Impostor," Naturejobs.com, http://www.nature.com/naturejobs/2009/090521/full/nj7245-468a.html.

Julie Morgenstern, *Time Management from the Inside Out: The Foolproof System for Taking Control of Your Schedule—and Your Life*, 2nd ed. (New York: Henry Holt, 2004).

Chapter 7: You Should *Not* Treat Everyone the Same

Myers-Briggs Foundation, "How Frequent Is My Type?," http://www.myersbriggs.org/my-mbti-personality-type/my-mbti-results/how-frequent-is-my-type.asp.

Center for Applications of Psychological Type, "Estimated Frequencies of the Types in the United States Population," http://www.capt.org/mbti-assessment/estimated-frequencies.htm.

Del Jones, "Not All Successful CEOs Are Extroverts," *USA Today*, June 7, 2006, http://www.usatoday.com/money/companies/management/2006-06-06-shy-ceo-usat_x.htm.

Adam M. Grant, Francesca Gino, and David A. Hofmann, "The Hidden Advantage of Quiet Bosses," *Harvard Business Review*, December 2010.

CHAPTER 8: Work Happy: Motivation That *Really* Matters, Boss

Sara L. Rynes, Barry Gerhart, and Kathleen A. Minette, "The Importance of Pay in Employee Motivation: Discrepancies Between What People Say and What They Do," *Human Resource Management* 43, no. 4 (Winter 2004): 381–94, available at http://bit.ly/kx1VXP.

Bob Nelson, *1001 Ways to Reward Employees* (New York: Workman, 1994).

Edward L. Deci with Richard Flaste, *Why We Do What We Do: Understanding Self-Motivation* (New York: Penguin, 1995).

Daniel H. Pink, *Drive: The Surprising Truth About What Motivates Us* (New York: Riverhead, 2009).

Paul P. Baard, Edward L. Deci, and Richard M. Ryan, "Intrinsic Need Satisfaction: A Motivational Basis of Performance and Well-Being in Two Work Settings," *Journal of Applied Psychology* 34 (2004): 2045–68.

Kenneth W. Thomas, *Intrinsic Motivation at Work: Building Energy and Commitment* (San Francisco: Berrett-Koehler, 2000).

Marcus Buckingham and Curt Coffman, *First, Break All the*

Rules: What the World's Greatest Managers Do Differently (New York: Simon and Schuster, 1999).

Chapter 10: You Can't Be Too Nice for a Tough Talk: Negative Feedback Is Necessary

Friedrich Försterling, *Attribution: An Introduction to Theories, Research and Applications* (Philadelphia: Psychology Press, 2001).

Chapter 11: Stop Fixing, Start Coaching

Roy Peter Clark and Don Fry, *Coaching Writers: Editors and Reporters Working Together Across Media Platforms*, 2nd ed. (New York: Bedford/St. Martin's, 2003).

Chapter 12: Change Is the New Normal: Lead the Way

Egdar H. Schein, *Organizational Culture and Leadership*, 4th ed. (San Francisco: Jossey-Bass, 2010).

John Kotter and Dan S. Cohen, *The Heart of Change: Real-Life Stories of How People Change Their Organizations* (Boston: Harvard Business School Publishing, 2002).

David M. Noer, *Healing the Wounds: Overcoming the Trauma of Layoffs*, revised and updated ed. (San Francisco: Jossey-Bass, 2009).

Lynda Gratton, *Hot Spots: Why Some Teams, Workplaces, and Organizations Buzz with Energy—and Others Don't* (San Francisco: Berrett-Koehler, 2007).

Jeffrey Pfeffer and Robert I. Sutton, *Hard Facts, Dangerous Half-Truths, and Total Nonsense: Profiting from Evidence-*

Based Management (Boston: Harvard Business School Publishing, 2006).

Chapter 13: What's It Really Like to Work Here, Boss?

Douglas McGregor, *The Human Side of Enterprise* (New York: McGraw-Hill, 1960).

Daniel J. Levi, *Group Dynamics for Teams*, 2nd ed. (Thousand Oaks, CA: Sage Publications, 2007).

Peter Drucker, *The Effective Executive: The Definitive Guide to Getting the Right Things Done* (New York: Harper Business Essentials, 2002 [first published 1967]).

Chapter 14: Management Is a Team Sport: How to Manage Your Boss, Your Deputies (and Even Your Stress)

John J. Gabarro and John P. Kotter, "Managing Your Boss," *Harvard Business Review*, January-February 1980.

Barbara Kellerman, *Bad Leadership: What It Is, How It Happens, Why It Matters* (Boston: Harvard Business School Publishing, 2004).

Robert I. Sutton, *The No Asshole Rule: Building a Civilized Workplace and Surviving One That's Not* (New York: Warner Business, 2006).

Chapter 15: For Great Bosses, It's Always About the Values

Lynn Sharp Paine, "Managing for Organizational Integrity," *Harvard Business Review*, March-April 1994.

Eric J. Romero and Kevin W. Cruthirds, "The Use of Humor in the Workplace," *Academy of Management Perspectives*, May 2006.

Katherine Karl, Joy Peluchette, Leda Hall, and Lynn Harland, "Attitudes Toward Workplace Fun: A Three Sector Comparison," *Journal of Leadership and Organizational Studies*, Winter 2005.

Robert K. Cooper and Ayman Sawaf, *Executive EQ: Emotional Intelligence in Leadership and Organizations* (New York: Perigree, 1998).

The Office, Season 3, Episode 22, "Beach Games."

Jim Naughton, "Why Fun Matters," Poynter Online, November 2002, http://www.poynter.org/uncategorized/3320/why-fun -matters/.

James M. Naughton, *46 Frogs: Tales of a Serial Prankster* (Wholly KOW Books, 2011).

About the Author

Jill Geisler is a senior faculty member of the Poynter Institute and heads its leadership and management programs. She holds a bachelor's degree in journalism from the University of Wisconsin and a master's degree in leadership studies from Duquesne University. She can be reached through her website, www.jillgeisler.com and followed on Twitter @jillgeisler.